ACTIFRANCE

Kate Beeching

Oxford University Press 1989

Oxford University Press, Walton Street, Oxford OX2 6DP

Oxford   New York   Toronto
Delhi   Bombay   Calcutta   Madras   Karachi
Petaling Jaya   Singapore   Hong Kong   Tokyo
Nairobi   Dar es Salaam   Cape Town
Melbourne   Auckland

and associated companies in
Berlin   Ibadan

Oxford is a trade mark of Oxford University Press

© Oxford University Press 1989

First published 1989

ISBN 0 19 912100 1

Acknowledgements

The author would very much like to thank Isabelle le Guilloux for
her help with the recording, John Beeching for the photographs
and also the great number of people who agreed to talk on the
cassette.

Illustrations are by Jan Lewis.

Cover photograph is by H. Wendler, The Image Bank.

Photographs are by Peter Downes p.53 and David Simson p.93.

All other photographs are by John and Kate Beeching.

The publishers would like to thank the following for permission
to reproduce copyright material.

Poitou Charentes (Comité Régional de Tourisme) p.13; Michelin
Tyre Public Limited Company pp.21,46; Thierry Calage p.30;
Bois de la Font p.32; UCRIF pp.37,38,40; Rennes Gaumont p.44;
le Groupement des Hôteliers, Vernet-les-Bains p.47; la Mairie de
Salies-du-Salat p.48; Safaraid Tourisme et Loisirs p.49; le Café
Lou Bolat p.58; Brittany Ferries p.62; Tourisme Verney pp.67,68;
Télérama p.77; Magazine *O.K!* p.85; FUAJ, p.95.

Although every effort has been made to contact copyright
holders, a few have been impossible to trace. The publishers
apologize to anyone whose copyright has been unwittingly
infringed.

Phototypeset by Tradespools Ltd, Frome, Somerset
Printed in Hong Kong

Contents

Introduction

What is Actifrance?

Actifrance is a collection of authentic documents, both spoken and written, drawn from a variety of sources – from a circus announcement to what the fashions are this year; from photos of signs and notices to personal letters.

Who is it for?

Texts were selected and activities devised with Basic Level GCSE and Foundation / General Level Standard Grade candidates in mind. The focus is on listening and reading comprehension and on spoken fluency.

How does it do it?

Actifrance helps you to understand contemporary spoken and written French and not to be 'fazed' by the things you don't understand. You will be given various tasks to perform which will involve you in the material – this, in its turn, will help you remember key-phrases and vocabulary. Spoken work will often be conducted in pairs with one of you asking for information and the other providing it – a real test of your powers of communication!

Finally, lots of colour and black and white photos bring France into your classroom and will make the activities more memorable.

In the words of one of my interviewees:
Bon appétit, bon voyage et bonne traversée!

Kate Beeching

1 Un sorbet à la banane

Qu'allez-vous prendre?

Look at the menu below and listen to the extract on the tape. You'll hear three French teenagers deciding what to eat and drink at the café. Write down what they order on a piece of paper. Note that Samuel forgot something when he summed up their order.

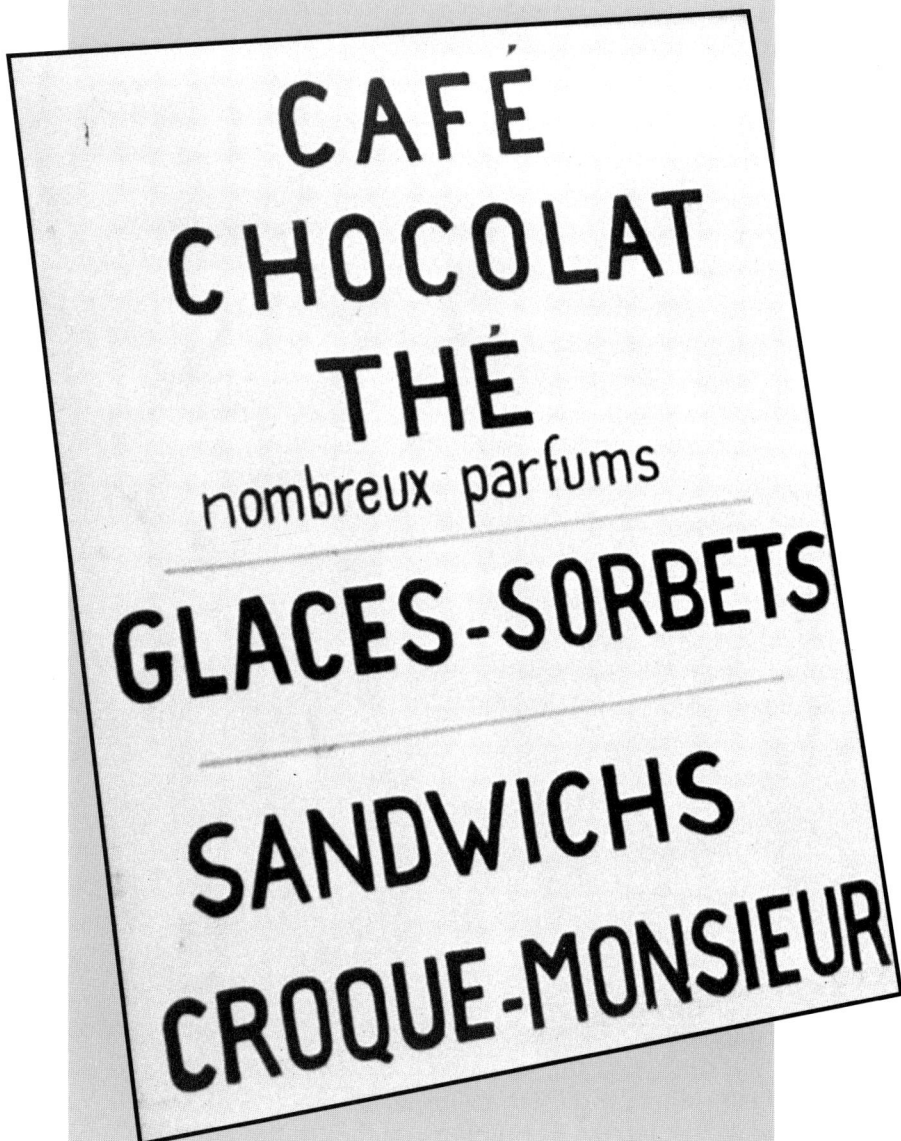

CAFÉ
CHOCOLAT
THÉ
nombreux parfums

GLACES-SORBETS

SANDWICHS
CROQUE-MONSIEUR

Qu'est-ce que c'est?

Look at the photos below. Each item is described on the tape but not in the same order as the photos on the page. Write the numbers 1–4 in a column on a piece of paper. Listen to the passages on the cassette and beside each number write down which photo you think best corresponds to what you have heard: a, b, c or d.

A

B

C

D

Listen again and list the ingredients you would need to make the **terrine de saumon** and the **croque-monsieur**.

Pair work

For this exercise you should work in pairs, one person sitting opposite the other. One person – Partner A – should look at the information on this page and will take the part of the waiter / waitress. The other person – Partner B – should turn the page and take the part of the customer.

Decide who is going to turn the page, then read on . . .

Partner A

- You are the waiter / waitress at the café.
- Your partner is going to ask you what kinds of ice-creams you've got and how much they are.
- Look at the photo below to give the information required.
- Read everything through first and if you don't know a word, look it up in the vocabulary list at the bottom of the page.
- Then he or she will want to buy a snack meal.
- Again, you will have to describe what is on the menu below and the prices of the various items.

Nous avons des glaces à la vanille, aux fraises etc.
Vous voulez | une glace simple ou une glace double?
              | une boule ou deux?
A quel parfum la voulez-vous?

Nous avons | des burgers, des plats garnis, des salades etc.
             | des saucisses frites, des œufs frites . . .

noisette: hazelnut   **merguez:** spicy sausage
pistache: pistachio   **chantilly:** whipped cream
plombières: tutti frutti **rillettes:** potted meat

Pair work

Partner B

- You're starving and you've got 25F to spend. First, you go past an ice-cream kiosk. Your partner is serving.
- Find out what flavour ice-creams he or she has got and then buy yourself one.

- Next, you want to buy yourself a snack meal. Your partner is the waiter or waitress.
- Ask what snacks are available and find out how much they cost.
- Make your choice and order your meal.
- Remember to check up how much money you have left out of your 25F before ordering your snack.

Qu'est-ce que vous avez comme | glaces?
                                                    | casse-croûtes?

C'est combien?
Je prendrai une glace à la vanille / au chocolat.
Une glace simple / double.
Une boule au chocolat et une boule aux pistaches.

un burger

des œufs plats

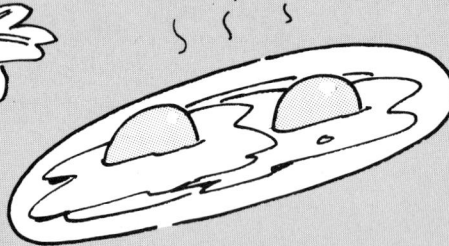

une glace double au chocolat et aux fraises

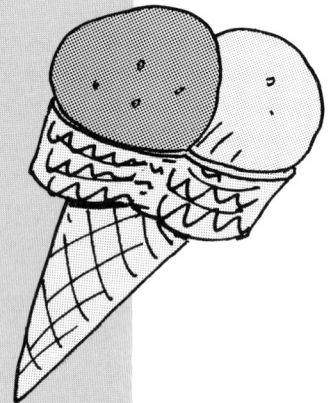

un steak haché frites

une salade de tomates

une glace simple à la vanille

2 C'est combien?

La poste

REPROMASTER 2.1

Listen to the conversation in the post office. Find out how much the stamps for each kind of mail cost. Write the prices on the letters on your worksheet.

La boulangerie

Listen to the conversation at the baker's van and look at the photos below. On the shopping list on your worksheet, tick the items I bought. Write in the price of each and check that your total is the same as that of the baker's girl.

REPROMASTER 2.2

Quel magasin?

Here are the things you want to buy . . . but where would you go to buy them? Write out your shopping list and write down the name of the shop you need in each case.

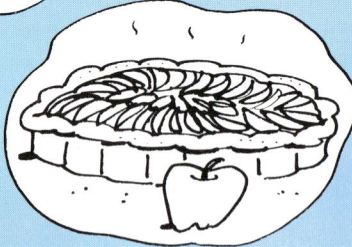

Pair work

You are at the market. Work with a partner who should sit opposite you. First one of you plays the stall-holder and the other the customer and then you swap roles.

First, decide who is to be Partner A and Partner B. Partner B should turn to the next page.

Partner A

Selling:

- Your partner will play the part of the customer first and will ask you whether you have the items on his or her shopping list.
- Look at the photos above and say whether you have the thing or not and its price.

Oui, combien en voulez-vous?
J'ai des . . . . . . à . . . . . . F ou à . . . . . . F.
   Lesquels / lesquelles préférez-vous?
Non, désolé, je n'ai pas de . . . . . .
Ils sont à . . . . . . le kilo / la pièce / le paquet.
Ce sera tout?
Ça fait . . . . . . F.

Buying:

- You've got a crowd of fruit-eating friends to feed. You want a melon, some grapes and masses of peaches or apricots.
- Ask your partner whether each fruit is available and how much it costs.
- Ask for the items which seem the best buy.
- Then, calculate whether the stall-holder is charging you the right amount of money! You'll need to write each thing down to check – or use a calculator.

Vous avez . . . . . .?
Ils/elles sont à combien?
Je prends un (demi-) kilo.
Je préfère les raisins | à . . . . . . F le kilo.
                       | noirs.
Je voudrais aussi des . . . . . . Vous en avez?
C'est tout. C'est combien?

Partner B

Buying:

- Your teacher will give you a shopping list such as you might be given by your host in France.
- Ask if the stall-holder (your partner) has the things on your list.
- Write down the price of each item and make sure that you are charged the correct amount at the end.

Vous avez . . . . . .?
Ils/elles sont à combien?
Je prends un (demi-) kilo.
Je préfère les courgettes à . . . . . . le kilo.
Je voudrais aussi des . . . . . . Vous en avez?
C'est tout. C'est combien?

Selling:

- Now your partner will play the part of the customer and will ask you for various things.
- Look at the photos below and say whether you have the thing or not and its price.

Oui, combien en voulez-vous?
J'ai des . . . . . . à . . . . . . F ou à . . . . . . F.
    Lesquels / lesquelles préférez-vous?
Non, désolé(e), je n'ai pas de . . . . . .
Ils sont à . . . . . . le kilo / la pièce / le paquet.
Ce sera tout?
Ça fait . . . . . . F.

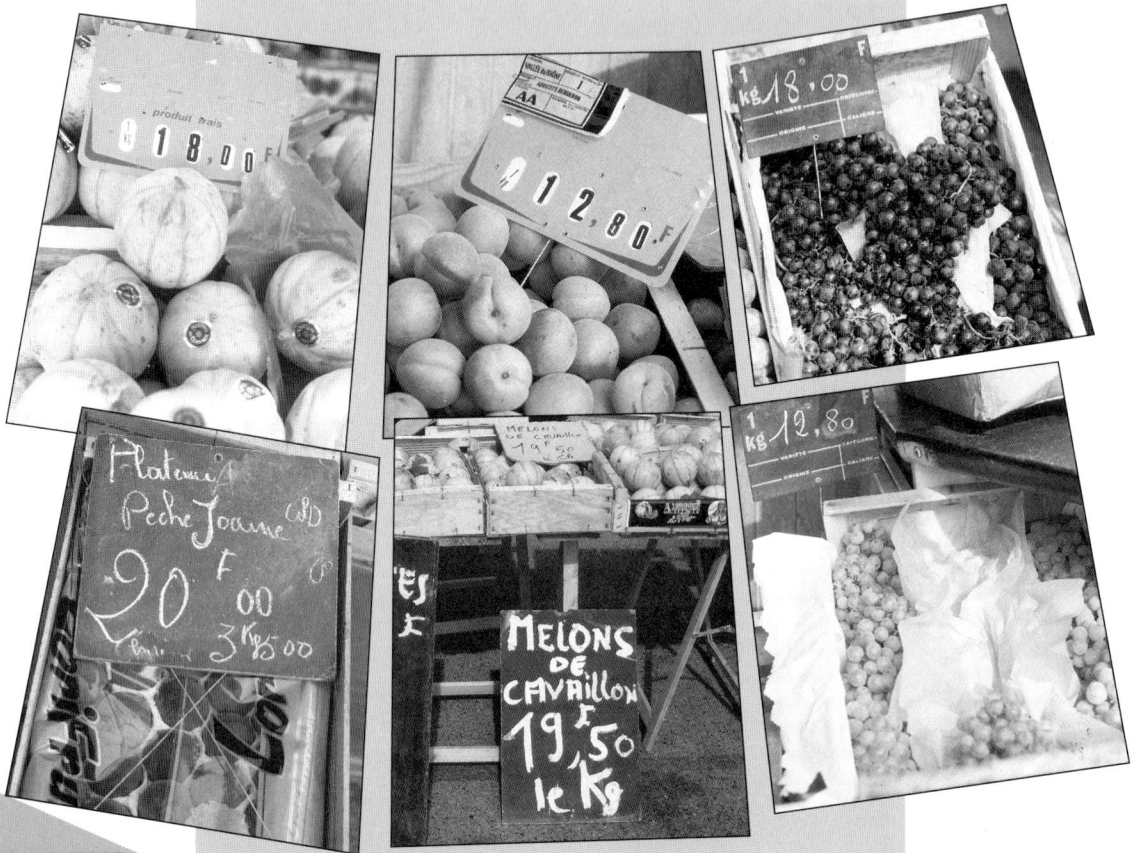

3 Camping Caravaning France

La liste des campings

If you ask at any **Syndicat d'Initiative** or **Office de tourisme** for **une liste des campings dans la région** you will be given a detailed list of all the camp-sites with information included according to a special key or **légende**, as you can see below:

Code postal, **COMMUNE** Camping caravaning, adresse	Capacité/Campeurs	■ à l'intérieur du camping □ à l'extérieur du camping ⛄🏕🛶🏊⚽🔥🍴🚿🛒🎣🚻🏪🚰🏠	Réservation	Période d'ouverture
79240 L'ABSIE				
Camping municipal, rue de Niort, tél. 49.63.80.50	42	□ □ □ ■ ■ □ □ □ □	■	15-06 au 15-09
16140 AIGRE				
Camping municipal « La Rivière »	40	■ □ □ ■	■	01-06 au 30-09
ANGLES–SUR–L'ANGLIN 86260 Saint-Pierre-de-Maillé				
Camping municipal « Les Côteaux », tél. 49.48.61.20	40	□ □ ■ ■ ■	■ •	01-02 au 30-10
16000 ANGOULÊME				
Camping municipal « Ile de Bourgines »	200	■ □ □ □ ■ ■ □ ■ □ □ □ □ ■ ■ •		toute l'année
17690 ANGOULINS				
« La Montée Sud », Fief de la Gare	390	□ □ □ □ ■ ■ ■ ■ □ □ □ □ ■ ■ •		

Guide Camping Caravaning du Comité Régional du Tourisme Poitou-Charentes.

REPROMASTER 3.1

Before looking at the details of the camp-sites, match up the symbols with the writing on the worksheet provided.

Now look back at the information about the two camp-sites above. You have to decide which camp-site you prefer. You should do this in the following way:

1 First put the amenities in order of preference depending on your needs and tastes.

2 At which camp-site can you . . .

a meet a lot of other campers?

b go swimming?

c do sports?

d have access to electricity and water?

e buy prepared food?

f book in advance?

3 Based on the detailed comparison you have made of the two camp-sites, write a short paragraph in English in which you say which one you would prefer to stay at and why.

Ce sont de véritables frites!

You are about to hear Mme Bellorge, the **propriétaire** of the **Camping des Govelins** talking about how much it costs to stay at the camp-site and what amenities are available.

Look carefully at the check-list on your worksheet. Study the price list and the other information given in the photos. Then listen to the passage in which additional information is given and fill in the details required on your worksheet.

REPROMASTER 3.2

Pair work

Work with a partner who should sit opposite you. Partner B should turn to the next page.

Partner A

- You are the person in charge at the **Camping la Truffière** near the rivers **Lot** and **Célé** in the **Massif Central.**

- Look carefully at the information given about the prices and amenities in the photographs below and answer your partner's questions.

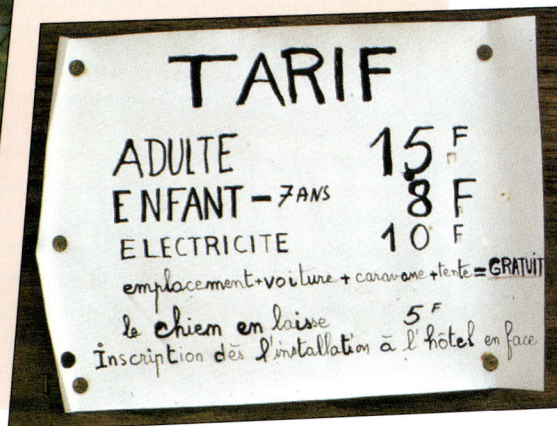

Pair work

Partner B

You want to stay at the **Camping la Truffière**. Your partner is the person in charge. Find out how much it costs to stay there and what amenities are available.

Quel est le tarif pour une nuit au Camping la Truffière?
Où est-ce que je dois m'inscrire?
Est-ce que vous avez de l'eau chaude?
Est-ce que vous avez un magasin sur place?
Est-ce qu'on peut . . . . . . faire du canoë / faire de l'équitation / jouer au tennis?
Est-ce que vous offrez de l'animation le soir?

Fill in the information on the worksheet provided.

REPROMASTER 3.4

JE CAMPE DANS LE LOT ET VOUS ..?

(65)
35.07.09

COMITÉ DÉPARTEMENTAL du TOURISME

SÉRIGRAPHIE JEANNETAUD CAHORS

4 J'ai des cheveux longs, bouclés et bruns

Je porterai une jupe blanche

Your pen-friend has sent you the letter below in which she describes what she looks like and what she'll be wearing when she arrives at the station. Unfortunately, you can't go to meet her. Write a note, as if for your mother or father – in English – in which you describe what Sandrine looks like so that they can go and pick her up from the station for you:

Bonjour

J'arriverai à la gare jeudi 13 à 18h00. Je porterai une jupe blanche et un polo vert. J'aurai une petite valise noire et un sac à dos jaune. Je suis de taille moyenne. J'ai les cheveux châtains et les yeux marron. A bientôt

Sandrine

C'est qui, Edith?

Listen to Edith describing herself on the tape.
Is she the girl in photo 1, 2 or 3? Listen carefully to the passage and write down your answer.

Student profiles

You're helping to organise a study tour for young French people in your home town. In order to help the teachers and the families who will be having the students to stay, you've decided to write a profile of each student. Listen carefully to the tape-recording again and note down the information required on your worksheet. You can start with Edith whose photo you have just identified.

REPROMASTER
4.2

Pair work

Work with a partner who should sit opposite you. Partner B should turn to the next page.

Partner A

Qui c'est?

- You've got photos of several people but you don't know who the people are.
- Describe each photo to your partner. He or she will be able to tell you who the person is and what they do for a living!
- Write the numbers 1–6 down the margin in your exercise book and for each photo write in the person's name and occupation.

Sur la photo 1, 2, 3, ... j'ai une femme/un homme . . . . . .

Elle/il a | une vingtaine / trentaine / quarantaine etc. d'années.
des cheveux gris / marron / noirs / blonds / frisés / bouclés.
des yeux bleus / marron / verts / noirs.
une barbe / des boucles d'oreille.

Elle/il porte | un gilet bleu clair / bleu foncé / noir.
une chemise blanche / bleue / rose.
des lunettes / un nœud papillon.

Comment s'appelle-t-elle / il?
Elle / il a quel âge?
Qu'est-ce qu'elle / il fait dans la vie?

Pair work

Partner B

- Your partner has some photos and you have incomplete descriptions of the people in the photos. You also have their names and occupations.
- Write the numbers 1–6 down the margin in your exercise book.
- Your partner will start by describing each of his or her photos. You should try to find the description below which best fits what your partner has said.
- Write the letter of the description beside the correct number.

If your partner has not given you enough information, you can ask questions like:

Est-ce qu'il porte des lunettes? Est-ce qu'il a des cheveux noirs? Est-ce qu'elle porte des boucles d'oreille? etc.

- After each photo, you should ask your partner for the missing information marked by '?' below and write it down in your exercise book.

A Georges Lefèvre
52 ans
Serveur de café
Cheveux gris
Lunettes?

B Jeanne Lamarck
45 ans
Marchande de vins
Cheveux courts, marron
Porte . . . . . . ?

C Jean-Pierre Lebrun
28 ans
Employé à l'agence de voyage
   'Nouvelles Frontières'.
Cheveux noirs, bouclés
Couleur des yeux?

D Anne Martin
23 ans
Hôtesse d'accueil chez Brittany Ferries
Cheveux noirs
Yeux noirs
Porte un pullover?

E Josiane Thierry
22 ans
Serveuse chez Brittany Ferries
Cheveux blonds / marron / courts
Yeux marron
Chemise blanche
Gros sourire?

F Yannick Laforge
38 ans
Steward chez Brittany Ferries
Cheveux noirs / un peu gris
Yeux marron
Chemise blanche, nœud papillon noir
Barbe?

5 Je continue tout droit, c'est ça?

You are about to visit the ancient city of Cahors. Look carefully at the map of Cahors on your worksheet.

Pour aller au Pont Valentré?

1 Listen to the conversation at the **Syndicat d'Initiative** where I asked for directions to:
**la cathédrale   le Pont Valentré   la gare S.N.C.F.
la banque la plus proche   la poste**
Trace the route to each given by the **hôtesse d'accueil** and write in the name of the place beside the appropriate number at the top of your worksheet.

REPROMASTER
5.1

VISITE DE LA TOUR DU DIABLE

HISTOIRE
AUDIO-VISUEL

Reproduced with the permission of Michelin from their Tourist Guide 'Périgord Quercy', 1st edition.

2 You are explaining to some non-French speaking friends what there is to see and do in Cahors. Read the questions below and listen to the passage again, looking at the map on your worksheet.

Then write down the answers so that you are ready to give your friends all the details.

a What would you see if you followed the route marked with arrows on your map – **l'itinéraire fléché**?
b What can you visit at the **Pont Valentré** and what are they showing at the moment?

c Why should you visit the **Mont St-Cyr**?
d How would you get there?
e What divides the medieval part of the city from **la partie plus aérée** – the more modern part with fewer buildings?

C'est indiqué...

Match up each phrase with the relevant photo:

On veut . . . . . . **a** faire de la natation
b garer la voiture
c pratiquer les sports nautiques
d acheter une pellicule
e déguster des vins
f faire de l'équitation
8 visiter une exposition d'art

Pair work

You're going to find out where everything is in the town of Salies-du-Salat. Work with a partner who should sit opposite you. Partner B should turn to the next page.

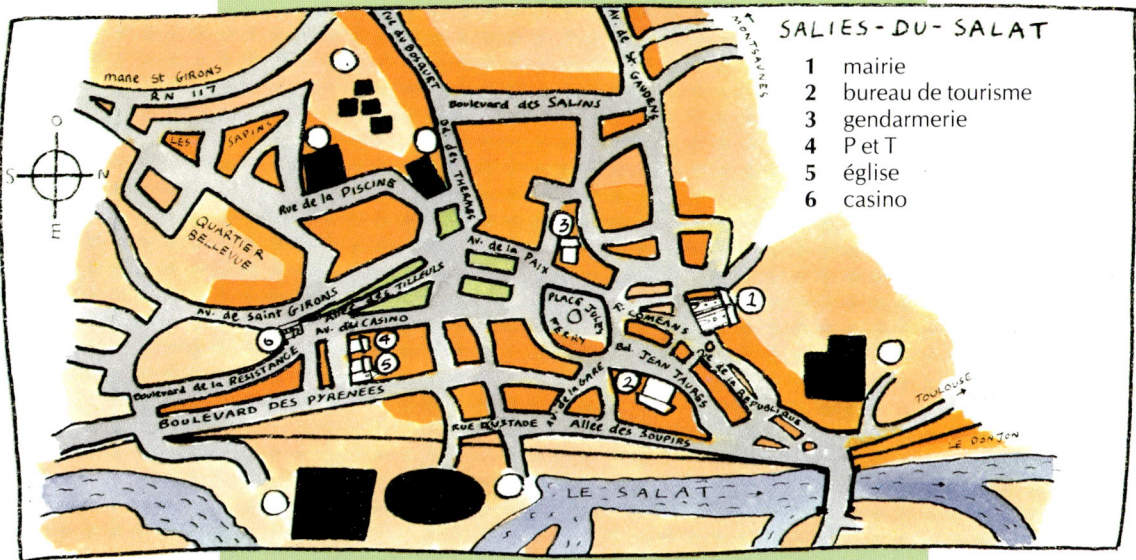

SALIES-DU-SALAT

1 mairie
2 bureau de tourisme
3 gendarmerie
4 P et T
5 église
6 casino

Partner A

Answering:

- You are visiting the small spa-town of Salies-du-Salat.
  You have half of the key to the plan above and your partner has the other half.
- You are standing in the middle of the **place Jules-Ferry** facing west.
- Give your partner directions to the places marked on your map (**1–6**).

Vous tournez à droite / gauche.

Vous prenez la rue . . . . . .

Vous prenez la première / deuxième rue à gauche / droite.

Vous continuez tout droit.

Le/la . . . . . . est | devant vous / à votre
                     | gauche / à votre droite.
                     | à l'angle de l'avenue
                     | . . . . . . et de la rue . . . . . .
                     | juste à côté de . . . . . .

C'est tout près d'ici.
C'est assez loin d'ici.

Asking:

- Now ask how to get to:
  the swimming pool
  the thermal baths – **les thermes**
  the camp-site
  the sports' ground
  the tennis court
  the ruined castle
- Write down the numbers 7–12 in your exercise book and, as you arrive at each place, write down its name against the appropriate number.

Pour aller au / à la / à l' / aux . . . . . . , s'il vous plaît?

Pair work

Partner B

- You are visiting the small spa-town of Salies-du-Salat. Your partner has half the key to the town plan below and you have the other half.

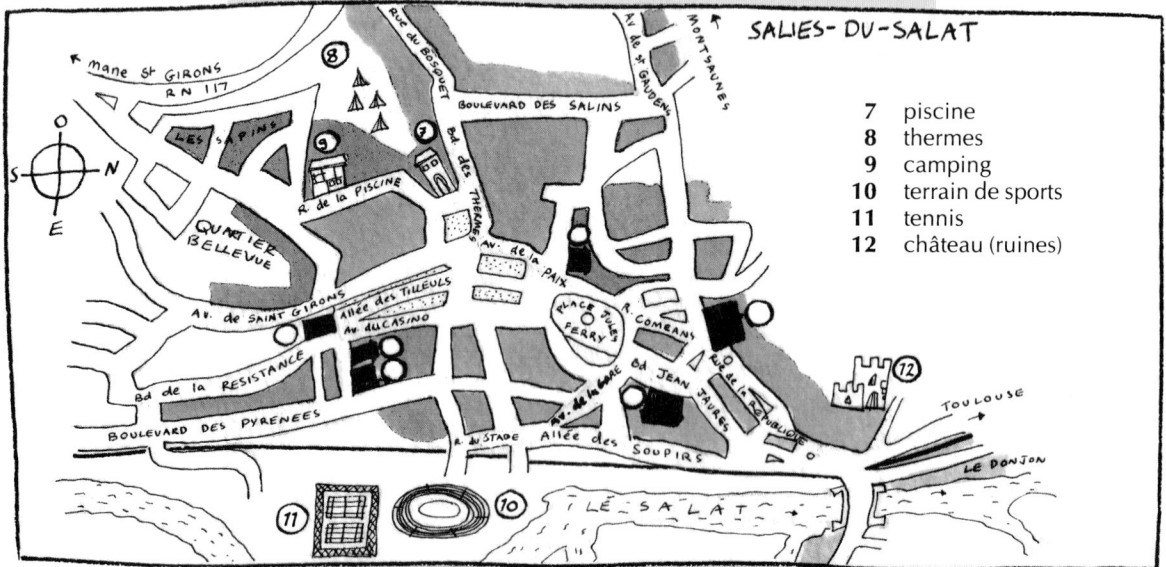

SALIES- DU-SALAT

7	piscine
8	thermes
9	camping
10	terrain de sports
11	tennis
12	château (ruines)

Asking:

- You are standing in the middle of the **place Jules-Ferry**, facing west.
- Ask your partner how to get to:
  the town hall – **la mairie**
  the tourist office
  la gendarmerie
  the post office
  the church
  the casino
- Write down the numbers 1–6 in your exercise book and, as you arrive at each place, write down its name against the appropriate number.

  Pour aller au / à la / à l' / aux . . . . . ., s'il vous plaît?

Answering:

- Now give your partner directions to the places marked on your map (**7–12**).

Vous tournez à droite / gauche.
Vous prenez la rue . . . . . .
Vous prenez la première / deuxième rue à gauche / droite.
Vous continuez tout droit.

Le/la . . . . . . est | devant vous / à votre gauche / à votre droite.
à l'angle de l'avenue . . . . . . et de la rue . . . . . .
juste à côté de . . . . . .

C'est tout près d'ici.
C'est assez loin d'ici.

6 Où se trouve la moutarde, s'il vous plaît?

Où se trouve...?

REPROMASTER
6.1

1 Listen to the employee at the supermarket explaining
where the items sketched below are to be found in the
shop and draw them in their correct position on the
supermarket shelves.

2 Which is the odd-one-out and why?

L'exception, c'est | le / la . . . . . . il / elle ne se trouve pas
avec . . . . . .
les . . . . . . ils / elles ne se
trouvent pas avec . . . . . .

Make up sentences like this, saying which is the
odd-one-out – **l'exception** – and why (because you
wouldn't find it with the . . . . . .).

oignon croissant poireau salade   l'alimentation
jambon melon charcuterie pâté   les conserves
carottes piles pain biscuits   les légumes
vin bière orangina viande   la coupe
sardines en boîte pâtes confiture   les boissons
   haricots verts en pot

Intermarché

You're going shopping at the supermarket . . . but how do you get your hands on a trolley – **un chariot?** And what do you do when you've finished with it?

Imagine you've been asked to provide the official English translation which will appear on all **Intermarché's** shopping trolleys throughout France! Write down your translation of the instructions in your exercise book.

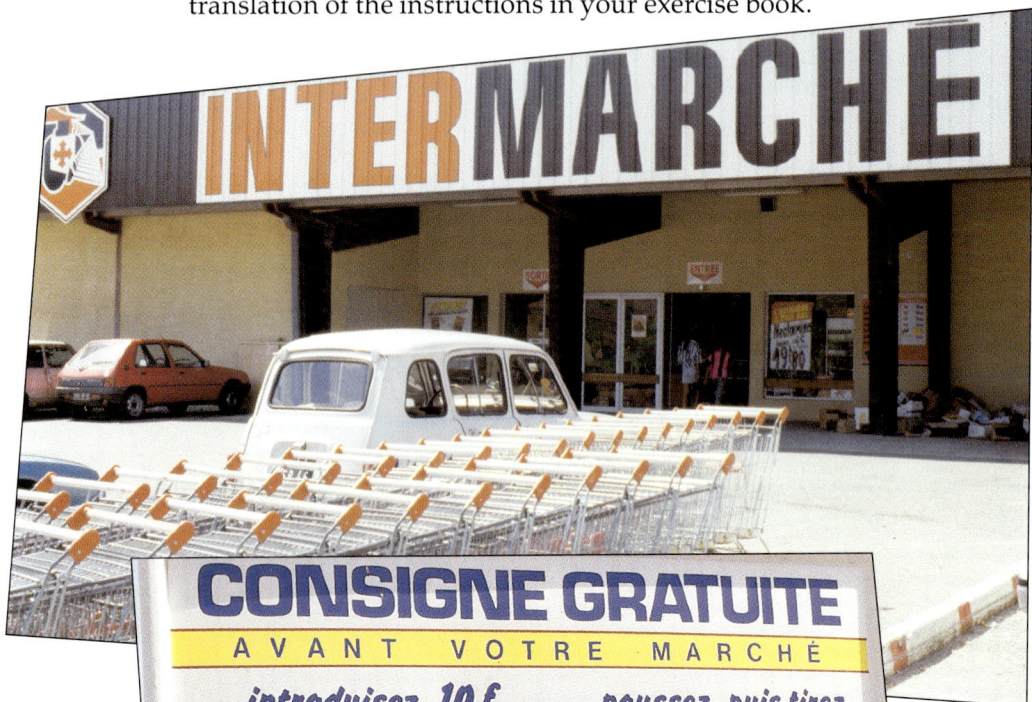

Pair work

You're going to do some consumer research. Work with a partner who should sit opposite you. Partner B should turn to the next page.

Partner A

Are supermarkets that much cheaper than the smaller shops?

- On this page you have photos which show the supermarket prices.
- Your partner has photos of prices in ordinary shops or service stations.
- First, ask your partner how much his/her petrol, pears and nectarines cost.
- Write down the prices.

L'essence est à combien?
Les poires sont à combien, le kilo?
Et les nectarines?

- Next, tell him/her how much the items cost at the big supermarket.

Now copy the grid below, filling in the different prices for the items listed.

	Supermarché	Petit commerce
20 litres de super		
Un kilo de poires		
Un demi-kilo de nectarines		
Ça fait:	F	F

Cross-check with your partner to make sure you have added up correctly!

Sum up your results by copying the sentence below into your exercise book, filling in the blanks correctly:

Ça revient . . . . . . (plus / moins) cher chez Intermarché par . . . . . . F.

Pair work

Are supermarkets that much cheaper than the little shops?

- On this page you have photos which show prices at the market or smaller family concerns.
- Your partner has photos of prices at the supermarket.
- First, tell him/her how much your goods cost.

brugnons nectarines

- Now, ask your partner how much his/her petrol, pears and nectarines cost. Write down the prices.

L'essence est à combien?
Les poires sont à combien, le kilo?
Et les nectarines?

Now copy out the grid below, filling in the different prices for the items listed.

	Supermarché	Petit commerce
20 litres de super		
Un kilo de poires		
Un demi-kilo de nectarines		
Ça fait:	F	F

Cross-check with your partner to make sure you have added up correctly!

Sum up your results by copying the sentence below into your exercise book, filling in the blanks correctly:

Ça revient à . . . . . . F (plus / moins) cher chez Intermarché.

7 Venez, venez, venez nombreux!

Bonjour, Christine!

Bonjour Christine, comment vas-tu? J'ai été très contente d'avoir reçu ta lettre. Elle m'a fait très plaisir. Il ne fait pas beau ici c'est comme chez toi mais j'espère que le soleil reviendra. Je ne suis pas très grande (1m52) j'ai 14 ans 1/2. Je suis désolée mais je t'enverrai une photo de moi la prochaine fois car je n'en ai pas encore. Envoie-moi aussi une photo de toi. Je vais me décrire, moi aussi: 1 m 52, 47 kilos, cheveux noirs, nationalité laotienne. Moi aussi je pratique beaucoup de sport: le basket, le volley-ball, le tennis, le hand-ball ... Oui, j'ai un hobby, je collectionne les timbres, les boîtes de cigarettes, vides bien sûr, des autocollants et des sacs en plastique. J'aime un peu le reggae, la new-wave, le rock'n roll, etc ... Bon je dois m'en aller, moi aussi je t'embrasse. Ecris-moi vite. Bye.

Ta correspondante Pathaim.

Pathaim is replying to Christine's letter.
Judging from what she says, what questions do you think
Christine asked her?

Quel spectacle?!

1 Look at the photos below. They correspond to the announcements you will hear on the tape but they are not in the same order.

Listen carefully to the extracts on the tape and then write down which order the items appear in.

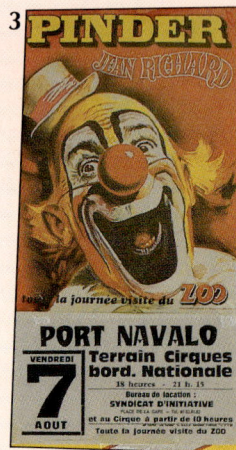

2 Look carefully at the photos above and at the information you need to fill in your worksheet. Fill in as much as you can from the information given in the photos. Then listen to the extracts on the tape once or twice more and fill in all the details.

REPROMASTER
7.1

Pair work

Work with a partner who should sit opposite you. Partner B should turn to the next page.

Partner A

- You're on the look-out for activities for young adolescents. You've heard about a **Parc de loisirs** called **Bois de la Font**. Your partner has all the details.
- Ask the following questions and fill in the information on your worksheet.

REPROMASTER 7.2

Qu'est-ce que vous offrez comme activités
   pour des jeunes adultes au Bois de la Font?
Est-ce qu'on peut y manger?
Quelles activités offrez-vous pour les enfants?
Quelles sont les heures d'ouverture?

- Now it's your turn to be in the know – look at the photo and see if you can work out what sort of museum the **Musée de plein air** is.
- Read the information and answer your partner's questions about it.

UNE BELLE JOURNÉE . . .
UNIQUE EN FRANCE!

Pour Déjeuner:
—l'excellent PLATEAU-REPAS SPÉCIAL-QUERCY au château
—votre pique-nique personnel dans le site même

Horaire:
Entrée de 10 h à 19 h.
Fermeture à 20 h.
Visite libre

prenez votre temps
vous pouvez revenir GRATUITEMENT pendant 8 jours!

OUVERTURE: tous les jours **sauf samedi** de juin à septembre (sur rendez-vous en avril-mai et octobre)

. . . DANS LE PLUS BEAU MUSÉE DE PLEIN AIR

On peut voir / manger . . . . . .
Il y a . . . . . .
Le musée est ouvert . . . . . .

Pair work

Partner B

- You run the **Bois de la Font** leisure park. Look at the information below and answer your partner's questions about it.

ATC adultes et enfants

golf miniature

promenades à poneys

crêperie-bar
pique-nique

restaurant-grill

toboggans nautiques

piscines chauffées
plage de sable fin
montagne molle

PARC DE LOISIRS

BOIS DE LA FONT

ouverture 1987 :
tous les jours de 10 h à 24 h
du 23 mai au 5 septembre

Varaire 46260 Limogne-en-Quercy
tél. : 65 24 32 70

réservation restaurant
tél. : 65 31 58 12

accès : D 911 de Cahors à Villefranche-de-Rouergue
entre Concots et Limogne-en-Quercy

Il y a . . . . . . / on peut . . . . . .
Le parc est ouvert . . . . . .

**REPROMASTER
7.2**

- Now it's your turn to ask the questions. You've heard of a **Musée de plein air**. Ask your partner for more information about it and fill in your worksheet.

Qu'est-ce qu'on peut voir au musée de plein air?
Est-ce qu'on peut y manger?
Quelles sont les heures d'ouverture?
Est-ce que le musée est ouvert tous les jours?

8 Un autorail jusqu'à Rennes

Les horaires de train

REPROMASTER 8.1

Look at the symbols on your worksheet. How quickly can you match them up with the words listed on the right?

Pair work

Work with a partner who should sit opposite you. You are going to take turns to give and seek information about the trains timetabled on your worksheets. You will both start by studying your timetables and making notes. Partner B should turn to the next page.

Partner A
S.N.C.F. Paris–St-Malo

- You work at the information office at the Gare de Montparnasse in Paris.
- Your partner has just phoned to ask for information about trains to St-Malo. It's a family who want to travel on Sunday 5th July. They would like to travel on a through train with family compartments, on which they can get something to eat.

- You have asked for a moment to check the timetables for the best train and then you'll phone them back.
- Look carefully at the timetable on your worksheet, including the notes for each train. Fill in the grid on your worksheet with the relevant information.
- Work out which is the best train for your client and fill in the time of its departure and arrival at the bottom of the grid.

REPROMASTER 8.2

Answering:
- Answer your partner's questions about the trains on your timetable.

Asking:
S.N.C.F. Lyon–Paris

It's Saturday. You are travelling on the train from Lyon to Paris with a friend who has broken his leg.

- You want a high speed train which would take a wheelchair and you'd like to be able to get something to eat.
- Fill in the grid on your worksheet with the relevant information for each train by asking your partner the following questions:

Est-ce que le train de (11.02) circule le samedi?
C'est un train grande vitesse?
Est-ce qu'il y a une voiture-restaurant?
Est-ce qu'il y a des facilités pour des handicapés sur ce train?
Le train de . . . . . . arrive à quelle heure, s'il vous plaît?

Did you and your partner agree about which was the best train?!

Pair work

REPROMASTER
8.3

Partner B
S.N.C.F. Lyon – Paris

- You work at the information office at the station in Lyon.
- Your partner has just phoned to ask for information about trains to Paris. He/she wants to travel on a Saturday on a high speed through train with facilities for a friend in a wheelchair. They want to be able to get something to eat.
- Look carefully at the timetable on your worksheet, including the notes for each train. Fill in the grid on your worksheet with the relevant information.
- Work out which train is the best for your client and fill in the time of its departure and arrival at the bottom of the grid.

Asking:

S.N.C.F. Paris –St-Malo

You and your family want to go from Paris to St-Malo on Sunday 5th July.

- You want to find a through train with family compartments, on which you can get something to eat. You phone the station at Montparnasse to find out which is the best train.
- Fill in the grid on your worksheet with the relevant information for each train by asking your partner the following questions:

Est-ce que le train de (07.05) circule le dimanche?
Est-ce que le train circule le 5 juillet?
Est-ce qu'il y a une voiture-restaurant?
Est-ce que c'est un train famille?
Le train de . . . . . . arrive à quelle heure, s'il vous plaît?

Did you and your partner agree about which was the best train?!

Answering:

- Answer your partner's questions about the trains on your timetable.

C'est indiqué

Find the photograph which gives the answer to each
question:

1 Où est la gare, s'il vous plaît?
2 On peut manger à la gare?
3 Où est-ce que je peux me renseigner?
4 Où est la consigne?
5 Le train part de quel quai, s'il vous plaît?
6 Il y a des casiers à consigne automatiques?

A

BAR RESTAURANT

B

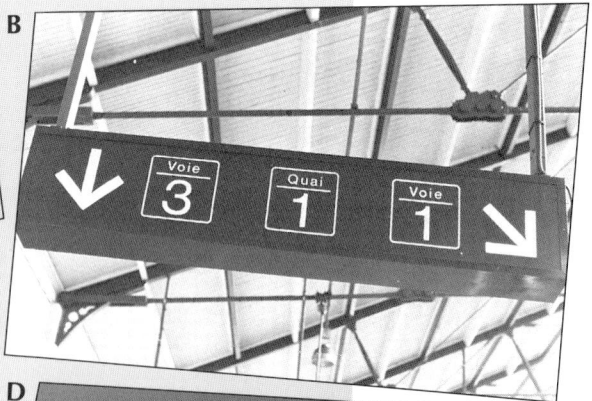

Voie 3 Quai 1 Voie 1

C

Gare S.N.C.F.
Centre Ville

D

Bagages Enregistrement Retrait

E

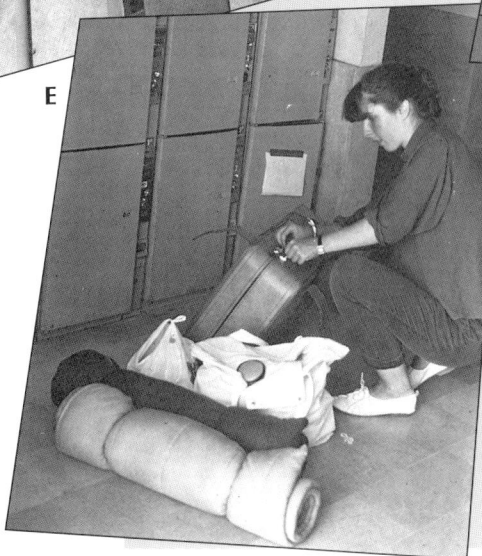

F

7455	2	22h55	TOULOUSE-Matabiau		RAP	12	4479		12h20
76	2	22h55 e	TOULOUSE-Matabiau Le Capitole		RAP	12	77		12h30
4409	1	23h00	PARIS-Austerlitz		EXP	12	4434	2	15h45
4430	2	23h08	AMSTERDAM	C S	RAP	12	5222	2	16h53
9236	2								17h20
4446	2	23h59	PARIS-Austerlitz		eXP	12	4424	2	
9628	2								

information réservation Billets

Un autorail à Rennes

You've just got off the cross Channel ferry in St-Malo and you want to get to St-Gildas-de-Rhuys on the Rhuys peninsula.

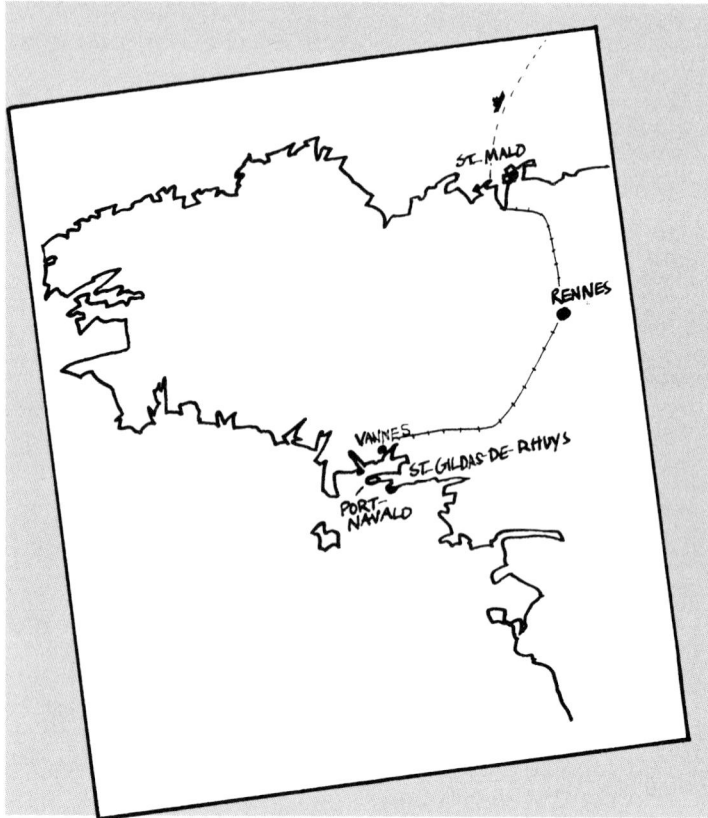

1 Listen to the passage on the tape and fill in the timetable on your worksheet.

REPROMASTER 8.4

2 Now listen again and answer these more detailed questions:

a How do you get from St-Malo to St-Gildas-de-Rhuys?

b Can you get anything to eat on the train?

c Which direction should you go in when you change at Rennes?

d Where do you buy the ticket for the trip between Vannes and St-Gildas?

e If you forgot to get off, where would you end up?!

9 Respecter le sommeil des autres

L'auberge de jeunesse de Rennes

1 Look at the table below which gives information about prices and facilities at the youth hostel in Rennes.

		A 135	1	2	3/4	5 et +	☕	✗	✗
34 ▲▲▲▲ ♿			43 F	43 F	33 F			10 F	32,5 F	75, 5F
Centre International de séjour Auberge de Jeunesse 10, 12 Canal St-Martin 35700 Rennes Tél. 99.33.22.33										

Now listen to the director of the hostel talking about how much it costs to stay there. The printers have got one of the prices wrong. Which is it?

2 Now listen again and answer these questions:

a How much does it cost to be a member of the youth hostelling association if you are:
under 18?
18–26 years?
over 26?
b How much does it cost to hire sheets? Can you take your own?
c Are hot meals only available in the evening?
d Why are showers included in the price?

3 Write down the French equivalents of the following English phrases. You will find these in the passage you have just listened to.

a How much does a room at the youth hostel cost?

b ...... francs in rooms with 3 or 4 beds, ... francs in rooms with 1 or 2 beds.
c There is a shower in every room.
d Is dinner included in the price per night?
e No, never. The meals cost ......, either at midday or in the evening.
f Are the showers included?

4 Look back at the symbols at the bottom of the extract about the youth hostel at Rennes. Answer these questions:

a Est-ce qu'on peut y nager?
b Qu'est-ce qu'on peut faire d'autre comme activités sportives?
c Est-ce qu'il y a un programme culturel?
d Ils offrent de l'animation le soir?
e Il y a des cours de langue?

Pair work

Work with a partner who should sit opposite you. You're going to swap information about two different youth hostels. Partner B should turn to page 40.

Partner A

- You have the information about the Centre Charles Péguy in Amboise and your partner has information about the Youth Hostel at Alpe d'Huez.

- Answer your partner's questions.

	A 63	1	2	3/4	5 et +	☕	✕	✕🛏
36 ▲▲ **Centre Charles Péguy** 1, rue Commire Entrepont BP 212 37402 Amboise Cédex Tél. 47.57.06.36	🛏	33 F	33 F	33 F	33 F	12 F	42 F	87 F

- Now look at your worksheet. Ask questions in order to find out how much it costs to stay at Alpe d'Huez and what activities are available.
- Use the questions and answers you wrote down in Exercise 3 on page 37.
- Fill in the information in the grid on your worksheet.

REPROMASTER 9.2

Savoir respecter la vie collective

We went on to ask the directeur at the **Auberge de jeunesse** in Rennes what rules they had at the hostel.

REPROMASTER 9.3

1 Listen carefully and look at the picture on your worksheet. Put a cross on the picture where a rule is being broken.

2 Listen again and find the correct ending to the phrases on the left from the list on the right. They give you the reasons for each of the rules.

a Pas de bruit après 22 heures –

b Il est interdit de fumer –

c On ne peut pas manger dans la chambre

d Il est interdit d'y laver son linge-

e Des auberges en milieu rural

1 acceptent des animaux.

2 pour des raisons d'hygiène.

3 il faut respecter le sommeil des autres.

4 on voit parfois des incendies.

5 il y a un endroit qui est prévu pour cela.

Pair work

Partner B

- Your partner has the information about the Centre Charles Péguy in Amboise. You have the information about the Youth Hostel at Alpe d'Huez.

- First, look at your worksheet. Ask questions in order to find out how much it costs to stay at the Centre Charles Péguy.
- Use the questions and answers you wrote down in Exercise 3 on page 37.
- Fill in the information in the grid on your worksheet.

50 ▲▲

Auberge de Jeunesse
Centre International de séjour
Chemin de la Coutte
38750 Alpe d'Huez
Tél. 76.80.37.37
Télex : 308449 F
Ouverture : du 1/12 au
30/04 et juil./août

	A 100	1	2	3/4	5 et +			
		57 F	57 F	57 F	57 F		40 F	110 F

- Now answer your partner's questions about Alpe d'Huez.

10 On pourrait aller au cinéma

Il paraît que c'est très marrant

REPROMASTER
10.1

1 Claire and Stéphanie are talking about what they can do on Saturday. They decide to go to the cinema. But which film do they choose in the end? Listen to their conversation, look at the advertisements for the films on your worksheet and tick the one they are going to see.

2 Now listen once again and answer these questions:

a Is the cinema near the house?
b What time is the film on?
c Where are the girls going to meet up?

3 Study the transcript carefully and find the French equivalents for the English phrases below. Write them down.

a What could we do on Saturday night?
b We could go to the cinema.
c I don't fancy it.
d 'Angel Heart' – do you know anything about it?
e I'd prefer to see an adventure film.
f Why not Crocodile Dundee?
g People say it's very funny.
h It doesn't look bad, this film.
i Yes, I'd like to go and see it.
j So, what time's the showing?
k Shall we meet at quarter to four?
l Yes, O.K.

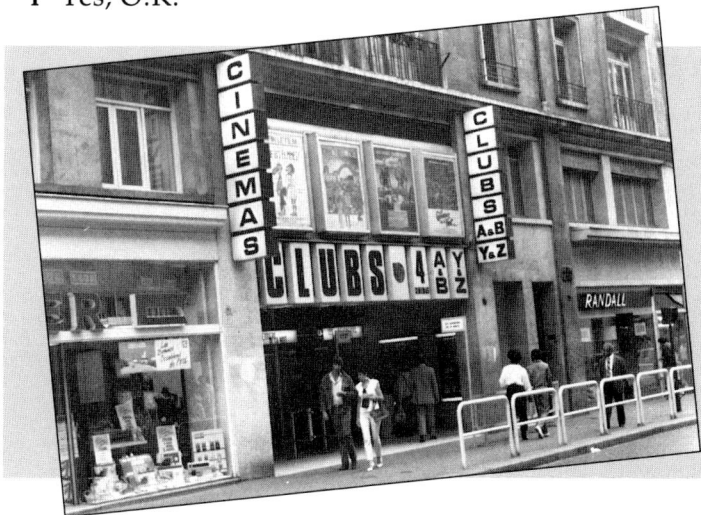

Pair work (1)

You're finding out about films on in Rennes. Work with a partner. Partner B should turn to page 44.

Partner A

- You've got the local newspaper. Read the information below and answer your partner's questions.

Les films au Gaumont

1
LE GRAND CHEMIN
Film français de Jean-Loup Hubert
14h 40   22F

2
LES ENFANTS DU SILENCE
CHILDREN OF A LESSER GOD
Film américain de Randa Haines
16h 30   25F

Cinéma Arvor
ANGEL HEART
Film américain d'Alan Parker
20h 30   35F 50

Cinéma Colombier
LE FLIC ÉTAIT PRESQUE PARFAIT
Comédie américaine de Michael Dinner.
18h 15   35F

ALAN PARKER
ANGEL HEART
AUX PORTES DE L'ENFER

WILLIAM HURT   MARLEE MATLIN
L'amour a son propre langage.
les **Enfants** du **Silence**
CHILDREN OF A LESSER GOD

LE BONHEUR EST DANS LE PRE...
...COURS-Y VITE !

JEAN-LOUP HUBERT
ANÉMONE
RICHARD BOHRINGER
le Grand Chemin

REPROMASTER 10.2

- Now help your partner who has received a letter from his/her pen-friend, Eric. Eric asks about films in Britain and your partner isn't sure what to reply. Discuss the letter and help write a reply.

Pair work (2)

Qu'est-ce qu'on pourrait faire samedi?
You and your partner are on holiday in the Lot. Look at
the advertisements below together. They show
things-to-do in and around Cahors.

- Using the phrases you have learnt from Claire and
  Stéphanie (Exercise 3 on page 41), discuss with your
  partner which activity you'd prefer.
- Come to an agreement about what you are going to do
  on Saturday.

LE RICHEMONT

BAR
salon de thé
dégustation
GALETTES . CREPES
PATISSERIES MAISON
COUPES GLACEES

La Vallée du Lot ou les causses avec sa monture.

mise en selle - promenades ou randonnées

Maury georges "Le Colombier" TOUR de Faure
Renseignements
Tel 31 27 43   de 13 à 14h ou après 20h
ou sur place

GROTTE du Pech Merle

Vente des tickets à la caisse du musée
Le nombre des visiteurs est limité
impérativement à 25 par guide.

LE CABANON RESTAURANT
* PÉDALOS * PÊCHE
* MINI . GOLF *
PRÈS DE
L'ÉCLUSE...

Musée de Saint Cirq Lapopie
Maison Rignault

UN SITE EXCEPTIONNEL
COLLECTION D' OEUVRES D' ART
EXPOSITIONS DE PEINTURE

Pair work

Partner B

You're finding out about films that are on in Rennes.

- Your partner has the local paper and is looking to see what's on.
- Fill in the missing information on your worksheet by asking your partner questions about the films.

'Les enfants du silence' se joue à quel cinéma?
La prochaine séance, c'est à quelle heure?
Ça coûte combien?

REPROMASTER
10.2

- Your pen-friend has sent you this letter and you're not sure what to reply. Show the letter to your partner and work out a reply together.

Cher John.

J'espère que tu as passé de bonnes vacances en France. As-tu visité Notre-Dame et la Tour Eiffel? A-t-il fait beau? Moi, j'ai passé mes vacances à St. Tropez. Il faisait très chaud et j'ai joué au tennis. Malheureusement, il n'y avait pas de cinémas! Vas-tu souvent au cinéma en Angleterre? Quels films as-tu vus ces derniers temps?

Ton ami Eric

11 Curiosités diverses

Sarzeau, c'est un petit bourg

1 The passage on tape tells you about the tourist attractions of Sarzeau and the Presqu'île de Rhuys. Study the map below carefully, listen to the passage and fill in the information on your worksheet.

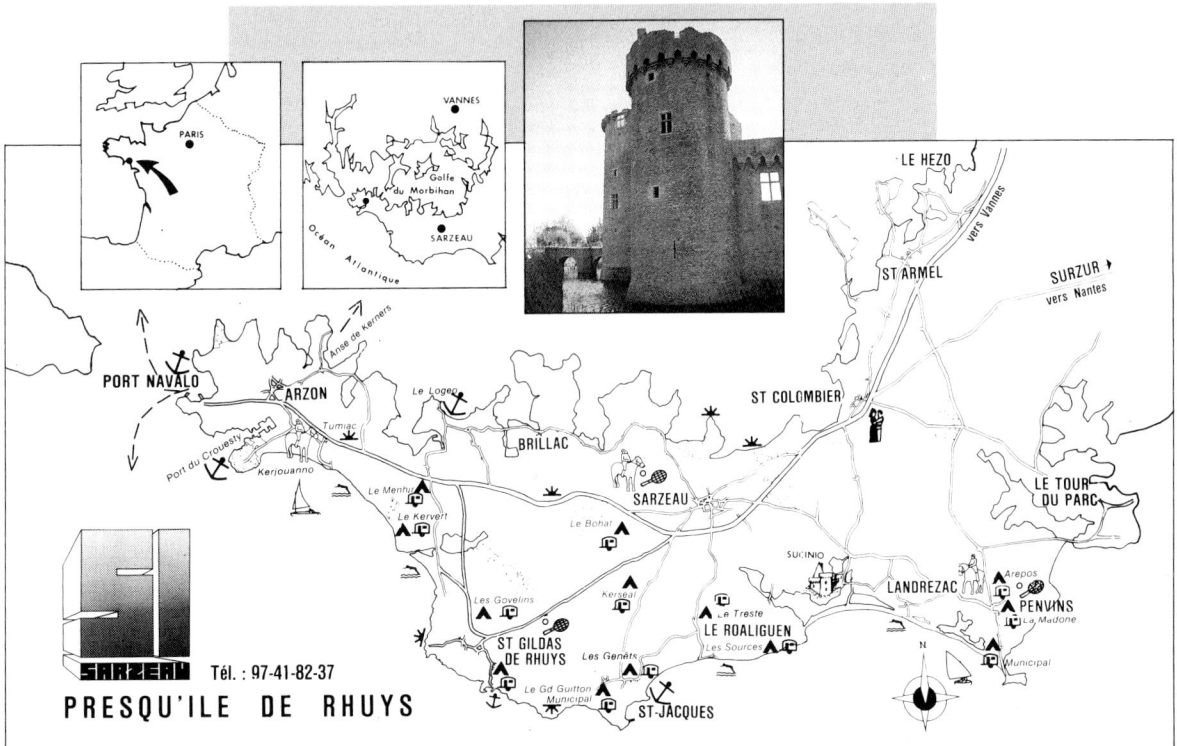

PRESQU'ILE DE RHUYS

Tél. : 97-41-82-37

2 Answer these more detailed questions about the passage:

a How far is the château from Sarzeau?

b What goes on during the festival de Suscinio?

c What makes the son et lumière show particularly spectacular?

d What sort of holiday could you have on the Presqu'île de Rhuys? What should you not expect to find there?

REPROMASTER 11.1

Visite à Brive-la-Gaillarde

You are spending one or two days in Brive-la-Gaillarde and want to spend half a day visiting the places of interest round about. Look at the map below, check what all the symbols mean in the key – **légende** – and decide on the best round trip. Write a detailed description in English of the places you'll visit.

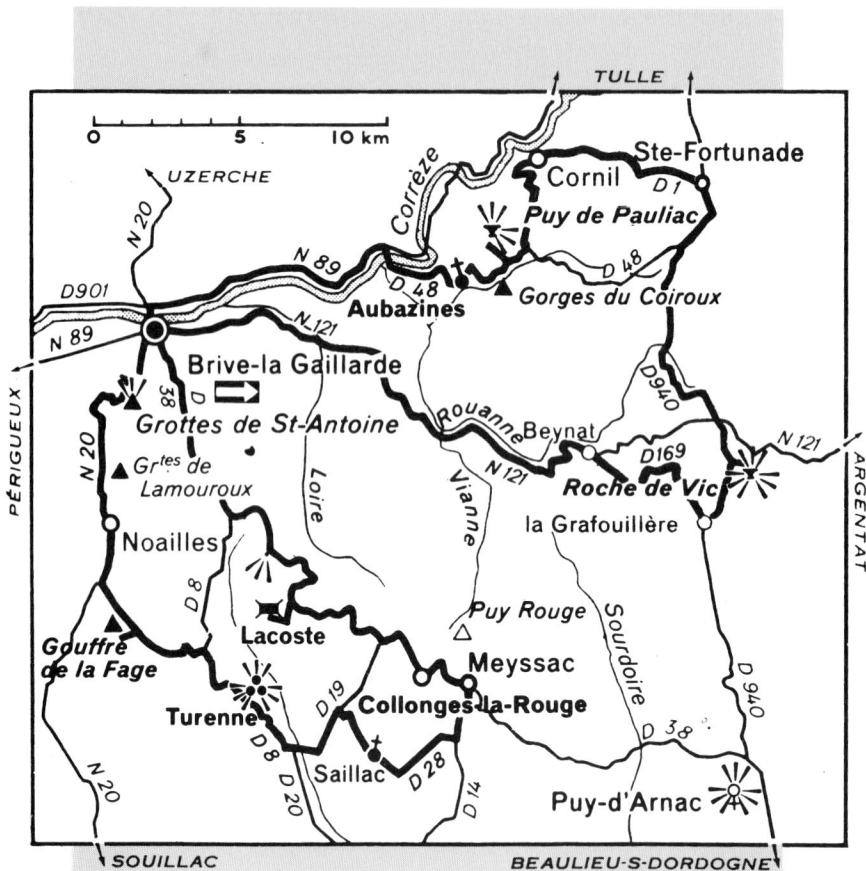

⋈	Château	⁂	Panorama
⁘	Ruines	⋎	Vue
⚲	Chapelle	▲	Curiosités diverses

Reproduced with the permission of Michelin from their Tourist Guide Périgord Quercy, 1st edition.

Pair work

You're going to swap information about two different spa-towns. Work with a partner who should sit opposite you. Partner B should turn to the next page.

Partner A

- You want to take your Mum or Dad for a **cure** (water-cure) at a French spa-town. You're comparing Vernet-les-Bains – which you have information about below – with Salies-du-Salat – which your partner has information about.
- First, read the information about Vernet and fill in the gaps on your worksheet.
- Then, answer your partner's questions about it.

UN EQUIPEMENT COMPLET POUR LES LOISIRS

—piscine publique chauffée indépendante de la piscine de l'établissement thermal (ouverte de juin à septembre)

—tennis, volley-ball, stade

—centre équestre avec manège couvert, promenades et poney club pour enfants

—excursions en jeep vers le Canigou et l'Abbaye de Saint-Martin

—night club, discothèque

—circuits pédestre balisés

—club de l'amitié: bridge, échecs, photos, bibliothèque, conférences.

- Finally, ask your partner to give you the information you need about Salies-du-Salat. Here are the questions you need:

Qu'est-ce que vous avez comme attractions touristiques à Salies-du-Salat?

Qu'est ce qu'il y a comme activités sportives?

Est-ce qu'il y a de l'animation le soir?

Fill in the information on your worksheet.

- Finally, looking at the details listed on your worksheet, talk to your partner about which place you'd prefer:

Je préférerais aller à Vernet/Salies parce qu'on peut aller à la pêche etc.

REPROMASTER 11.1

Pair work

Partner B

- You want to take your Mum or Dad to a health resort at a French spa-town. You're comparing Salies-du-Salat – which you have information about below – with Vernet-les-Bains – which your partner has information about.

- First read the information about Salies-du-Salat below and fill in the gaps on your worksheet.

SALIES du SALAT
31260 Haute-Garonne

ETABLISSEMENT THERMAL Municipal

OUVERT DU 2 MAI AU 30 SEPTEMBRE—LES EAUX LES PLUS MINERALISEES D'EUROPE

FEMMES **ENFANTS** **TOUS ADULTES**

Bains · Douches · Sauna

Distractions dans la Ville

TENNIS (5 courts dont 1 couvert)—CIRCUITS Pédestres et Cyclistes
PROMENADES à Cheval—PECHE (lac et rivière)—PETANQUE—LES BORDS DU SALAT
CASINO: Boule, Cinéma, Night-Club

SALIES-DU-SALAT

au coeur de sites préhistoriques, historiques, archéologiques et spéléologiques

à moins d'1 h de Toulouse par la voie rapide (75 km)

- Now ask your partner about Vernet-les-Bains. Here are the questions you need:

Quelles sont les attractions touristiques de Vernet-les-Bains?
Qu'est-ce que vous avez comme activités sportives?
Qu'est-ce que vous avez comme animation le soir?

Fill in the information on your worksheet.

- Next, answer your partner's questions about Salies-du-Salat.
- Finally, looking at the details listed on your worksheet, talk to your partner about which place you'd prefer:

Je préférerais aller à Vernet/Salies parce qu'il y a une discothèque etc.

12 En pleine action!

Safaraid – tourisme et loisirs

Safaraid is an exciting organisation which sets up canoeing trips down the river Dordogne in France – and in Africa too!

You are promoting the firm in England and they have sent you the brochure below.

Look at it and, using your worksheet to help you, design the English version of the brochure.

Descente de la Dordogne en Canoë-Kayak

Choisissez votre point de départ, votre point d'arrivée et la durée de votre circuit.

- **Tous les jours en juillet en août,** sur demande en juin et septembre.
- **Location libre à l'heure, à la journée,** à la semaine ou à la quinzaine.
- **Services Safaraid sur demande.**
  - Retour tous les soirs par bus.
  - Transport de vos bagages au point suivant.
  - Location de tentes bi-places et de bidons étanches.
  - Réservation des emplacements de camping
  - Descentes accompagnées tous les jours (sur demande).

- **INFORMATIONS et RESERVATIONS**
  SAFARAID – ALBAS - 46140 LUZECH Tél. : **65 36 23 54**
  19400 - Argentat en saison Tél. : **55 28 80 70** (du 15/6 au 15/9)

- A nos 9 points de location sur la Dordogne.
- A l'aide du bulletin d'inscription ci-joint.

REPROMASTER 12.1

Quel sport?

You are going to hear four passages in which four sports are being talked about. But which passage goes with which picture(s)?

Mark your answer on your worksheet.

A

B

C

D

Pair work

Work with a partner who should sit opposite you. Partner B should turn to the next page.

Partner A

- You've received this letter from your pen-friend who is due to arrive in England later this year. Talk to your partner about the letter and about what sports you are all quite good at and could play together.

Bonjour!

Mon prénom est Fabien. J'habite à Paris. J'espère que tu pourras comprendre ce que je t'écris. A Paris tout va bien; moi, je suis un sportif, je fais du basket, du foot, du tennis et de la natation. En hiver, je skie à la montagne. Mon groupe de musique préféré est "Téléphone". Je mesure 1 m 65, j'ai 13 ans et j'en aurai 14 au mois d'Octobre. J'espère que tu me répondras vite. A bientôt.

Fabien

Tu es un sportif, toi?
Tu aimes nager, faire du basket etc.?
J'aime bien ...... – c'est un de mes sports favoris.
Tu es doué(e) au foot?
Moi, je ne suis pas du tout doué(e) au tennis.
Je ne sais pas faire du ski.

- Your partner has a sporting proposal for you! Decide whether you fancy it.

Pair work

Partner B

- Your partner has received a letter from his/her pen-friend in which he describes what sports he likes. Discuss what sports you are good at and what you might play together.

Qu'est-ce qu'il fait comme sport?
J'aime bien . . . . . . c'est un de mes sports favoris.
Tu es doué(e) au tennis, toi?
Moi, je ne suis pas du tout doué(e) au basket.
Tu sais faire du ski?

- Your pen-friend has written asking whether you and a friend would like to come skiing at Chamonix next year. Read her letter (below) and describe what it's like to your partner.

  Talk about how good you are at skiing and whether you'd like to go.

Salut,
Je t'écris de Chamonix où je passe de magnifiques vacances dans les Alpes. Je fais du ski de fond et j'adore ça. Il fait un soleil splendide et j'ai déjà beaucoup bronzé. L'hôtel est très confortable et tous les matins, on nous apporte le petit déjeuner au lit et à midi et le soir on fait de très bons repas. Je fais aussi un peu de ski alpin mais avec des skis de fond. J'aime bien m'élancer sur les pentes enneigées. Bon, maintenant, il faut que je te quitte car on frappe à la porte, cela doit être la serveuse qui apporte le petit déjeuner. Je t'embrasse, Véronique

13 Un paquet-cadeau

Mont St-Michel

You're spending a couple of hours at Mont St-Michel before getting on the night-boat back to England.

Where should you park? Beside sign post 1, 2 or 3?

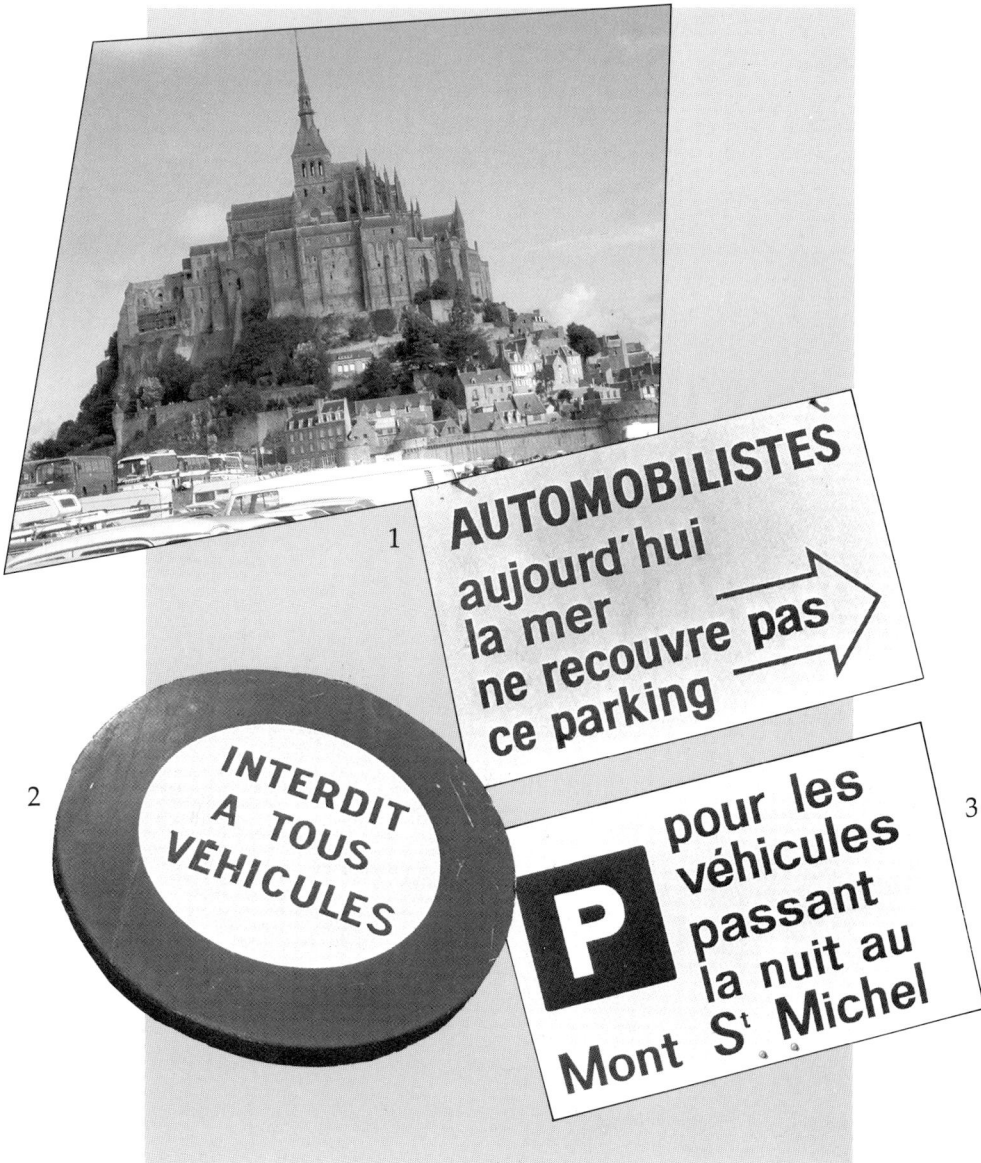

1

AUTOMOBILISTES
aujourd'hui
la mer
ne recouvre pas
ce parking

2

INTERDIT
A TOUS
VEHICULES

3

P pour les
véhicules
passant
la nuit au
Mont St Michel

Une poupée bretonne

1 Look at the photos below, listen to what Isabelle buys at the **Ti Breiz (la maison bretonne)** in Rennes and fill in your worksheet.

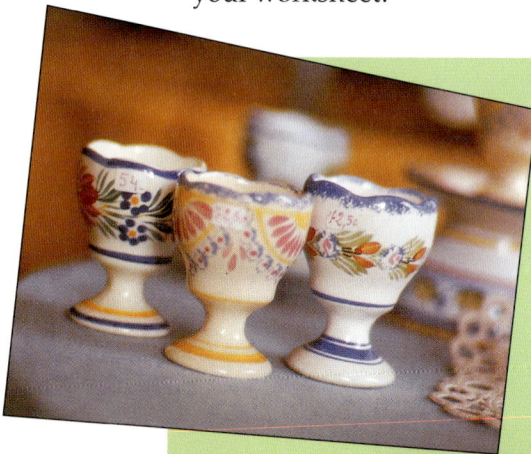

2 Copy out the sentences below. Listen to the tape and fill in the blanks.

    a Isabelle veut acheter un cadeau pour une petite fille de . . . . . . ans.

    b Elle prend . . . . . .

    c Elle voudrait quelque chose en . . . . . . pour une jeune femme de 16,17 ans.

    d Elle s'appelle . . . . . .

    e Le bol coûte . . . . . .

REPROMASTER 13.1

Pair work

You're in a souvenir shop. Work with a partner who should sit opposite you. Partner B should turn to the next page.

Partner A

Take turns to be the customer and the employee.

Buying:
Your partner is selling souvenirs. You've got 150F left.

- You want to buy some postcards or colour slides (**des diapos**) of Mont St-Michel.
- You also want some advice on what to buy for your Dad and for your kid-sister (aged 6).
- And you're starving! Ask what there is to eat!
- At the end of the day make a detailed list of what you've bought and how much it all came to.

Selling:
You are selling the items shown in the photos below.

- Tell your partner the price of each item.

F56.00   F18.00   F40.00

Pair work

Partner B

Take turns to be the customer and the employee.

Selling:
You are selling the items shown in the photos below.

- Tell your partner the prices and give advice on what to give his/her father and young sister (the coquilles Saint-Jacques contain sweets – **des bonbons!**).

Buying:
Your partner is selling souvenirs. You have 100F to spend.

- You want some post-cards, a hair-band, a bracelet and some Breton pottery.
- You can buy all these things from your partner – but check the prices first!
- At the end of the day, make a detailed list of what you've bought and how much it all came to.

14 Nous faisons des crêpes

Quel restaurant?

You want to have a quick snack. Look at the menus outside the cafés below and decide which looks the most suitable place to go. With a partner, act out the conversation in which you order your snack.

Menu Estival

SALADE FRAICHEUR

OMELETTE de la MÈRE POULARD
cuite au grand feu de bois

MOUSSE AUX FRUITS DE SAISON

95 frs Prix net   Boisson non comprise

1er & 2ème ETAGES

BAR CREPERIE
service à toute heure
Dégustation
Fruits de mer
Omelette
Sandwichs
Glaces
en coupe
Mystère
Mont-Rose
cassates
parfaits
fruits givrés
liégeois
Pâtisseries
Cidre bouché

MENUS DU JOUR

ENTREES AU CHOIX:
Crudités du Jardin
Terrine Maison
Maquereau Frais au Vin Blanc
PLATS AU CHOIX:
POULET ROTI Pommes Frites
CARRÉ DE PORC Légumes et Pommes Frites

DESSERTS AU CHOIX:
Glace du Jour
Mousse au Chocolat
Pâtisserie Maison
45 Frs

ENTREES AU CHOIX:
Omelette «POULARD»
Salade composée du jour
6 Huitres du Cotentin
PLATS AU CHOIX:
AGNEAU ROTI et sa Garniture
ESCALOPE DE VEAU à la Normande
BROCHETTE DE POISSON GRILLÉE AU FEU DE BOIS

DESSERTS AU CHOIX:
Tarte aux Pommes
Ile Flottante Crème Anglaise
Coupe Glacée
85 Frs

TAXES ET SERVICE COMPRIS
SERVICE CONTINU DE 11H. A 21H. 30

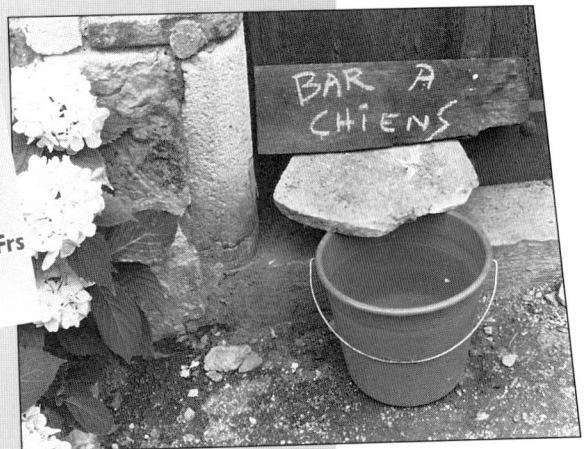

BAR A CHIENS

Quel plat?

1 You're in St-Cirq Lapopie near Cahors.
Listen to M. Péchoin, proprietor of the Lou Bolat café
describe the main dish on the menu today.

   a Which dish in the photos below is he describing?

   b Complete the following sentence: Service continu de
. . . . . . à . . . . . .

A

B

C

D

Lou Bolat
BAR   CAFÉ
Place de la Poste

TERRASSE PANORAMIQUE

Restauration de qualité

Crêpes repas
Crêpes dessert

San "pastis" servi tiède
sur table

TÉL. 65 30 29 04

AUX BONS PRODUITS
DU TERROIR

● Ses grands vins de Cahors
sélectionnés

● Ses produits régionaux
des meilleurs artisans,
conserveurs du Lot

● Ses Prix compétitifs

TÉL. 65 30 29 56

2 Listen to the rest of the conversation with M. Péchoin.

   a Make a list – in English or French – of as many things
on the menu as you can.

   b Why does he particularly recommend 'Lou Bolat'?

Pair work

You're in a restaurant. Work with a partner who should sit opposite you. Partner B should turn the page.

Partner A

Customer:

- Study the menu carefully. If you do not know what any of the dishes are, ask the waiter or waitress. Then order your meal.

Qu'est-ce que c'est, le/la/les . . . . . .?
Qu'est-ce que c'est, le plat du jour aujourd'hui?
Je prends . . . . . .
Et ensuite, ...
La note, s'il vous plaît.

- At the end of the meal, the waiter or waitress will give you a bill. Check that they've got it right!

Pair work

Partner B

Waiter/waitress:
- Quite a few English people come into your restaurant. Your boss has given you a list of what the dishes are in English but unfortunately they've got muddled up!
- Pair each one up on your worksheet so that you're ready to answer your partner's questions when he/she comes in to order a meal.

Le plat du jour – today's special – is **cassoulet**; a tasty stew made with pork and beans.

REPROMASTER 14.1

Bonjour, qu'est-ce que vous prenez?
Et ensuite?

La note? Oui, j'arrive tout de suite.

- Write down your partner's order and give him/her a bill at the end.

15 Bon appétit, bon voyage et bonne traversée

A quelle heure part le ferry, s'il vous plaît?

You are taking the crossing from Portsmouth to Caen-Ouistreham and then back again. (If you're not sure where these places are, look at the map on the next page!)

Listen to the four short extracts on the tape.

1 – is the announcement you hear as you get into your bunk on the night-boat leaving Portsmouth for France.

2 – is what you are told at the information office at Ouistreham on your return trip.

3 – is the conversation at the café on the boat, when you buy some French pâtisserie – shown in the photos on the next page!

4 – is the announcement you hear as this boat leaves for England.

Fill in the missing information on your worksheet.

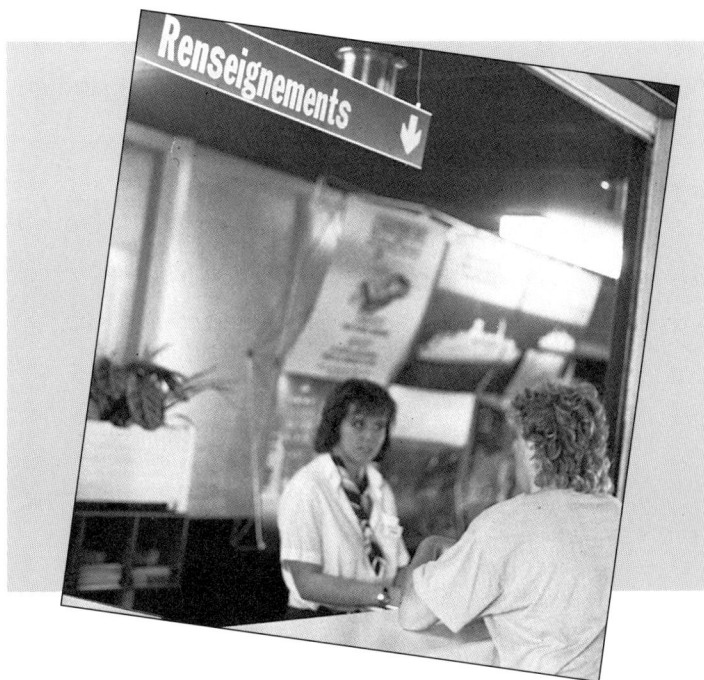

REPROMASTER
15.1

Brittany Ferries

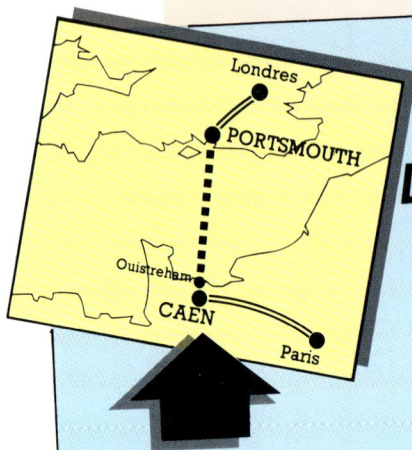

CAEN: LE NOUVEAU PORT DE PARIS POUR L'ANGLETERRE.

Caen, n'est qu'à 238 km de Paris par l'autoroute la plus verte de France, l'autoroute de Normandie A13.

Et à deux heures de Paris Saint-Lazare par le turbotrain.

Caen-Ouistreham/Portsmouth, la nouvelle ligne Brittany Ferries vous emmène en Angleterre toute l'année, de jour ou de nuit, sur un nouveau bateau "Le Duc de Normandie" qui chaque jour peut transporter 1500 passagers et 360 voitures dans un confort de "croisière".

Read this description of Brittany Ferries' new line from Portsmouth to Caen. Fill in the information you need on the check-list on your worksheet.

A glimpse inside the cafétéria on the Duc de Normandie:

REPROMASTER
15.2

Pair work

Work with a partner who should sit opposite you. One of you should turn the page.

Partner A

Answering:

- Your partner wants to buy some last-minute presents before getting on the ferry. You are the shop assistant. Give advice about what he or she could buy. Here is what you have on offer:

Write out a receipt – **un récépissé** – for the things your partner buys.

Asking:

- You're at the port. You want to find your way to:
  le bureau de change   les toilettes   le bureau de renseignements   la sortie   le contrôle billets de Brittany Ferries   le contrôle douane   le départ pour les passagers piétons
- You also want to know what time the Prince de Bretagne (ferry) arrives and what time the boat leaves for Jersey.
- Ask your partner questions and fill in the answers on your worksheet.

Pair work

Partner B

Asking:

- You're on your return trip to England and you have 50F left.
- You want to buy some last-minute presents for your mother, your sister and – if there is any money left – yourself!
- Your partner is the shop assistant. Ask advice and act out the conversation in which you buy the presents.
- Ask for a receipt – **un récépissé** – for what you buy and work out how much money you have left.

Answering:

- Your partner wants to know the way to various places at the port and get some information about boat arrival and departure times.
- Look at the photos below and say which way to go (à gauche, tout droit, à droite) and the relevant times.

16 Une journée à Jersey

Tourisme Verney

Isabelle le Guilloux went in to the **Tourisme Verney** office in Rennes to find out what day excursions were on offer.

1 Listen to the tape and fill in your worksheet with all the details.

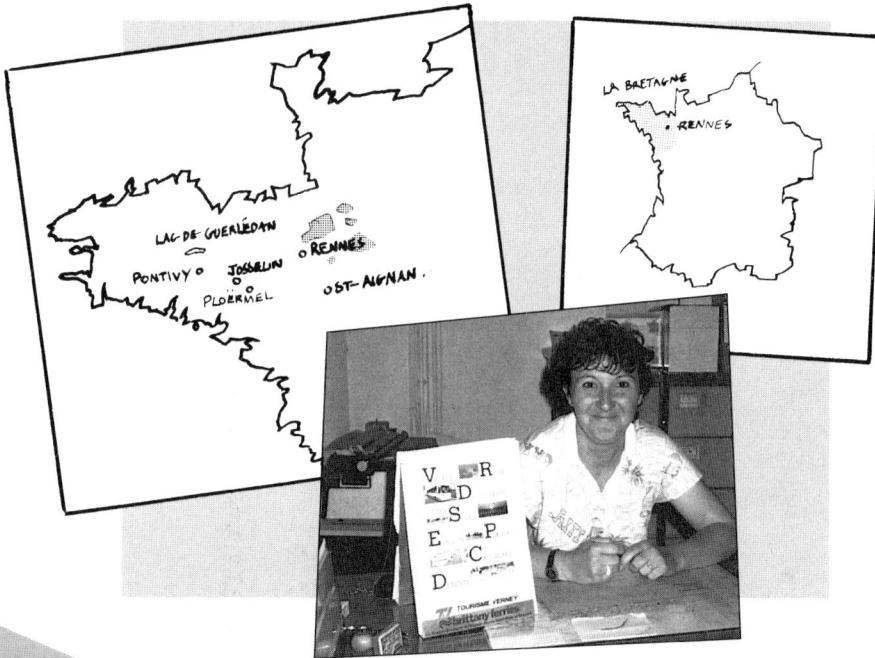

REPROMASTER
16.1

2 Listen to the passage once more and write down how Isabelle says:

   1 I'd like some information about excursions, please.
   2 What time does it leave in the morning, please?
   3 And how much is it, please?

3 Ecoutez une autre fois le passage et notez en français vos réponses aux questions suivantes:

   1 C'est une excursion pour groupes? – ou pour groupes et individus?
   2 L'excursion aura lieu à quelle date?
   3 Est-ce que l'autocar prend des passagers en dehors de Rennes?
   4 Est-ce que la boisson est comprise dans le prix?

Make the connection

Look at the photos below and see how many you can pair up or join together in a sequence.

A CHIEN MÉCHANT

B POUSSEZ

C P LIMITÉ A 1 HEURE

D Durée limitée à 1 heure
30 Minutes - 1 F
60 Minutes - 2 F
Pièces
JAEGER

E PRIORITÉ À LA VOIE MONTANTE
LE MONTAT
BALS GRATUITS
21 AOÛT: ROCKFELLER
12: EXPÉRIENCE

F CONTROLE DOUANE ET POLICE EMBARQUEMENT
CUSTOMS AND POLICE CONTROL EMBARCATION
ZONE SOUS DOUANE
ENTRÉE INTERDITE A TOUTES PERSONNES ÉTRANGÈRES AU SERVICE

G SITES ET MONUMENTS HISTORIQUES
Fontaine des CHARTREUX R.N. 20
Piscine Couverte Stade Croix de Fer
Centre de Stages et de Tourisme C.S.T
1 Km.
LUZECH
Visite de la Ville

K TELEPHONE

H BRITTANY FERRIES St MALO PORTSMOUTH
EMERAUDE FERRIES St MALO JERSEY GUERNESEY
CONTROLE BILLETS TICKETS CONTROL

I CETTE CABINE PEUT ÊTRE APPELÉE A CE NUMÉRO:
65 30 1168

J SECURITE
Un coup de fil peut sauver une vie
Respectons le téléphone public
PTT TELECOMMUNICATIONS

L CAR FERRY
ANGLETERRE
PRINCE DE BRETAGNE
ARRIVEE 8H15
ST MALO 30 AOUT
DEPART 10H45
ARMORIQUE 30 AOUT
ARRIVEE 19H50
DEPART 21H15
JERSEY&GUERNESEY SOLIDOR
8 00
DEPART 16H 20
30 AOUT
ARRIVEE 16 00
22 00

M 5F 2F 1F 1/2F

N TIREZ

O moi je dois rester dehors

Pair work

You're going to swap information about two different excursions. Work with a partner who should sit opposite you. Partner B should turn to the next page.

TOURISME VERNEY

SAMEDI 27 JUIN

Départ de RENNES Gare Routière a 12 h 45, pour ANGERS: arrêt devant le chateau – route des bords de Loire jusqu'à SAUMUR.
Dégustation de vins de Saumur chez ACKERMANN.
Dîner à SAUMUR.
Vers 22 h, spectacle son et lumière au chateau de Saumur.
Un voyage fantastique à travers le temps.
Après le spectacle, retour à RENNES. Arrivée vers 3 h du matin.

PRIX PAR PERSONNE:
285 Francs pour les adultes
240 Francs pour les enfants de moins de 10 ans.

CE PRIX COMPREND:
– le transport en autocar de grand tourisme
– le dîner, boisson comprise
– la dégustation de vins
– le spectacle son et lumière au chateau de Saumur

Partner A

You have the information about an excursion to Saumur and your partner has information about another excursion.

Asking:
- Your partner will be the person behind the desk at the information office first. You want to go to Jersey for the day. Ask questions to find out:
  a what is available
  b what you'll see or do
  c how much it costs
- Note down on a piece of paper in French or English as many details about the excursion as you can.

Je voudrais des renseignements sur des excursions à Jersey, s'il vous plaît.
Qu'est-ce qu'on fait pendant cette journée?
Quel est le prix?

Answering:
- Now you're the person behind the desk at the tourist office. Your partner wants to find out about excursions for individuals. Give him or her as much information as you can.

Pair work

Partner B

You have the information about an excursion to Jersey and your partner has information about another excursion.

Answering:
- You're the person behind the desk at the tourist office. Your partner wants to find out about day trips. Give him or her as much information about the trip to Jersey as you can.

SHOPPING A JERSEY

Départ de **Rennes** à 6 heures pour **Saint-Malo.** Embarquement à bord du **Solidor.** Départ à 8 heures. Arrivée à **Jersey** à 9 h. 30. Transfert à **St-Hélier** pour shopping. Déjeuner. Après-midi, tour de l'Ile. Embarquement à 17 h. 30 (heure locale). Arrivée à **Saint-Malo** à 21 h. 30, **Rennes** à 23 heures.

prix **385 F.** comprenant :
Le transport en autocar de grand tourisme, les traversées maritimes, le déjeuner, sauf boisson et le tour de l'île en autocar.
Possibilité de dîner à bord au retour : supplément **75 F.**
Formalités :
carte nationale d'identité en cours de validité obligatoire.

Asking:
- Now you want to find out about excursions to Saumur suitable for individuals. Ask questions to find out:
  - a what is available
  - b what you'll see or do
  - c when you leave and when you come back
  - d the price and what is included
- Note down on a piece of paper in French or in English as many details about the excursion as you can.

Je voudrais des renseignements sur des excursions pour des personnes individuelles, s'il vous plaît.
Quelles sont les attractions de cette excursion?

Le départ est à quelle heure?
On rentre à quelle heure?

Quel est le prix?
Ce prix comprend quoi exactement?

17 On va monter au premier étage

Juste à côté de la porte d'entrée

1 Listen to the conversation in which Isabelle talks about her parents' house in Rennes. Fill in the names of the rooms or pieces of furniture which are missing from the plan of the house on your worksheet.

REPROMASTER 17.1

2 Recopiez les phrases en remplissant les blancs:

   a En montant au premier étage, la lumière est . . . . . . (à gauche/à droite?).

   b Je peux laisser mes affaires de toilette . . . . . .

   c On peut transformer le canapé . . . . . .

   d La grande table a des rallonges pour faire . . . . . .

   e Le congélateur se trouve . . . . . . Pour tous les jours on a . . . . . .

   f Au sous-sol on conserve . . . . . .

   g La buanderie, c'était . . . . . .

Quel hôtel?

Which of the hotels advertised below would you prefer to stay at and why?

Je préférerais loger à l'hôtel . . . . . . parce que
j'aime bien . . . . . .
je n'aime pas . . . . . .

Hôtel de France ☆☆ NN
RESTAURANT REPUTE
24 CHAMBRES TOUT CONFORT
GARAGE INTERIEUR
TERRASSE FLEURIE
37600 **LOCHES**
6, rue Picois
Téléphone : (47) 59-00-32

= HOTEL - RESTAURANT =

BEAU-RIVAGE

l'Hôtel au bord de l'eau
Terrasse - Parc - Canotage
Tél. (45) 20.31.26

★★
Hotel
Restaurant

Le mur du roy

Bar-Terrasse avec vue sur la mer
Fruits de Mer et spécialités de poissons.

Penvins
(Presqu'île de Rhuys, 25 km de Vannes)
Tél. 97.67.34.08

GARE
SNCF
PTT
Calvos
Lalbenque
10 km
←Hôtel WILSON
H.W
Paris
Sarlat
Brive
RN 20
Montauban
Toulouse
Agen
MAIRIE
Rodez
Figeac
LE LOT
VIEUX CAHORS

Wilson
★★★

CAHORS

36 chambres avec bains, TV couleur, sono, minibars
Salle de réunion pour conférences et séminaires
Sauna Finlandais
Parking privé
Ouvert 24 h sur 24 h
▼

Hôtel Wilson
★★★

Centre Ville près Mairie
72, rue Président-Wilson
46000 CAHORS
Tél. 65.35.41.80
Télex : 699 886 F

Pair work

Work with a partner who should sit opposite you. Partner B should turn to the next page.

Partner A

● Describe the room below so that your partner can mark in the furniture on his or her worksheet.

En entrant par la porte, tu as en face de toi . . . . . .
A gauche / à droite tu trouveras le / la . . . . . .
A côté du / de la / de l' / des . . . . . . , il y a . . . . . .
Derrière la porte / près de la fenêtre, tu as . . . . . .

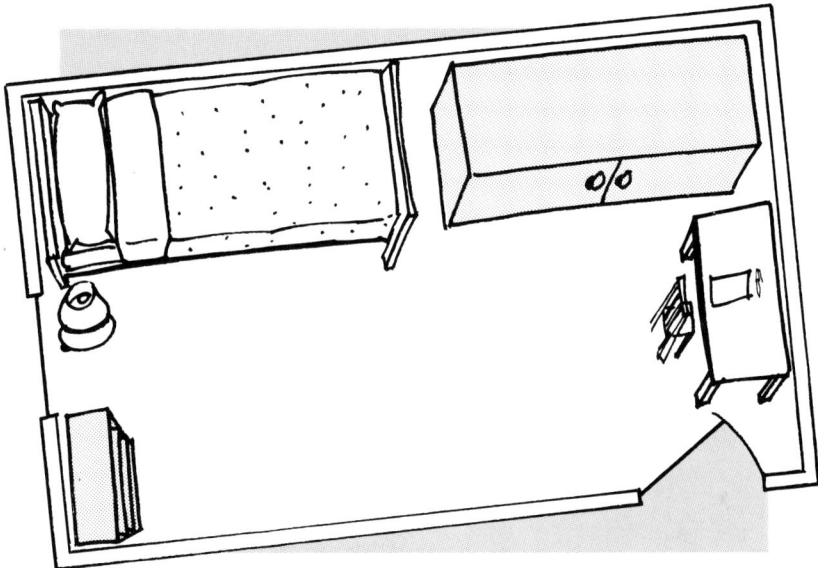

● Now fill in your worksheet according to the information given by your partner.

You can ask questions like:

La lampe de chevet est | entre le lit et les étagères, c'est ça?
à côté de l'armoire?
près de la porte?

A droite ou à gauche?

● Finally, check how well you've understood and made yourself understood by comparing the picture on your worksheet with the one on the next page!

Pair work

Partner B

- Listen to your partner telling you where the furniture is in his or her picture and mark it in in the correct place in the room on your worksheet.

You can ask questions like:

L'armoire se trouve à | côté du lit?
| près de la fenêtre?
A gauche ou à droite?

REPROMASTER
17.2

- Now describe the room below so that your partner can mark in the furniture on his or her worksheet:

En entrant par la porte, tu as dans le coin au fond . . . . . .
A droite, il y a . . . . . .
En face de toi, à côté de . . . . . . , tu as . . . . . .
A gauche / derrière la porte / près de la fenêtre, il y a . . . . . .

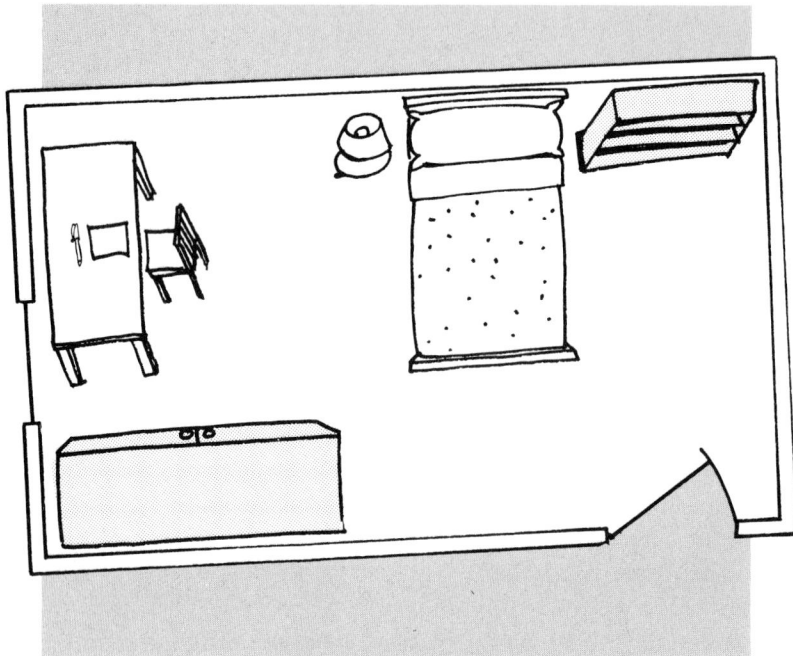

- Finally, check how well you've understood and made yourself understood by comparing the picture on your worksheet with the one on the previous page!

18 Du lundi au samedi soir

Des messages

Read the messages below and pair them up with the correct symbols on your worksheet.

1   Maman,
Je vais voir Christine
et je vais aller en
ville m'acheter un
pantalon. A ce soir.
Gros bisous.
    Laurence.
P. S : Dis à Fred de ne pas
toucher à mes cassettes.

2   Briac a
téléphoné -
il voulait
faire un tennis.
Il te rappellera
demain dans la
journée.

3   Va chez ton oncle.
C'est lui qui a les clefs de
la porte.

4   Sylvie viens vite.
J'ai besoin de toi,
je suis au bar, on va
faire un flipper !

5   Va faire les courses.
Prends du pain.

6   Je suis partie au
cinéma.
Je reviens vers
quatre heures.

7   Mon copain est venu me chercher
pour aller pêcher.

8   Il y a un message pour toi
sur le répondeur téléphonique.

Je vends du camembert

REPROMASTER
18.2

1 Listen to the extract on the tape and fill in the details on your worksheet.

2 Répondez aux questions:

   a Le réveil sonne à quelle heure?
   b Qu'est-ce qu'il y a sur les rayons 'produits frais'?
   c Est-ce que le directeur du supermarché travaille le samedi?
   d Combien de semaines de vacances a-t-il par an?
   e Depuis quand est-ce qu'il n'a plus de vacances?
   f Est-ce que sa femme commence à six heures et demie le matin?
   g Est-ce qu'elle aime ce qu'elle fait?

Pair work

Work with a partner who should sit opposite you. Partner B should turn to the next page.

Partner A

- You and your partner decide to go and learn French in France. You attend a French school and your partner decides to go and work in a baker's. You're trying to work out when you'll both be free to meet up.
- Look at your timetable below:

EMPLOI DU TEMPS

	lundi	mardi	jeudi	vendredi	samedi
8h15 à 9h15		gym			espagnol
9h15 à 10h10	math	gym	français	espagnol	h. géo
10h30 à 11h20	anglais	h.géo	h. géo	math	français
11h20 à 12h15	français		math	dessin	français
14h00 à 15h	sc. nat	français	gym		
15h à 16h	sc. phy	math	espagnol	anglais	
16 à 17h	musique	anglais		sc. nat / sc. phy	

h.géo. = histoire-géo(graphie): humanities
sc.nat. = sciences nat(urelles): biology
sc.phy = sciences phy(siques): physics

- Your partner is checking his/her working hours.
- Work out when you have free time to do things together. Say things like:

Quand est-ce que tu es libre?
Moi, je suis libre entre . . . . . . heures et . . . . . . heures le matin / tous les jours / vendredi.
J'ai des cours ⎰ lundi / mardi / mercredi etc.
Je n'ai pas de cours ⎱

- Write down the times when you are both free.

Pair work

Partner B

- You and your partner decide to go and learn French in France. You go to work in a French baker's and your partner attends a French school. You're trying to work out when you'll both be free to meet up.
- Look at the opening hours of the baker's below:

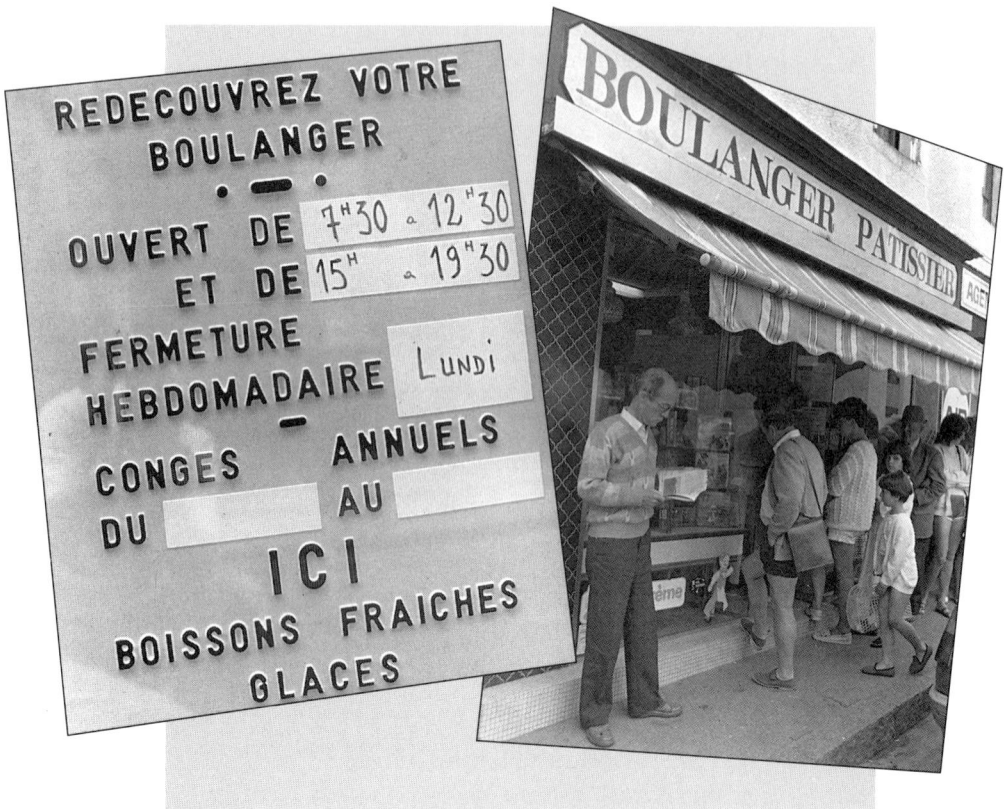

- Your partner is looking at his/her timetable.
- Work out when you have free time to do things together.

Say things like:

Quand est-ce que tu es libre?

Moi, je suis libre entre . . . . . . heures et . . . . . . heures le matin / tous les jours / vendredi.

Je travaille | lundi / mardi / mercredi etc.
Je ne travaille pas |

- Write down the times when you are both free.

19 Allez! On branche la télé

Quel programme?

Claire and Sandrine are babysitting. They're checking what's on television in **Télérama**, the French version of the Radio or T.V. Times.

REPROMASTER 19.1

1 Listen to their conversation and tick the programmes they decide to watch on your worksheet.

2 Match up the English phrases with their French equivalents on your worksheet.

REPROMASTER 19.2

3 Répondez aux questions en français:

a Quelle heure est-il?

b L'émission de dessins animés, comment s'appelle-t-elle?

c Les jeunes filles aiment-elles des films du genre 'Double assassinat dans la rue Morgue'?

d Quels autres genres d'émissions n'aiment-elles pas?

e Claire, suit-elle la série 'Dynastie'?

f A quelle heure vont-elles se coucher?

Petites annonces

You're looking for a pen-friend. Look through the small ads below. They appear every week in the teenage magazine **Podium-Hit**. Make a list of possible pen-friends – people who seem to share your interests. Then fill in the coupon on your worksheet for your own free advert – **petite annonce gratuite** – to appear in the next copy of the magazine.

* Petites Annonces *

ACHATS VENTES

Recherche documents et posters concernant Samantha Fox. Durieux Fabìenne, 1783 chemin de l'Escours, 06480 La Colle-sur-Loup.

*

Je recherche posters et photos sur des chanteurs rocks. Méchin Pénélope, 4 avenue Carnot, 08000 Charleville Mézières.

*

Je recherche posters ou documents sur Romy Schneider. Foucaud Thierry, PN 30 rue de Crouël, 63000 Clermont-Ferrand.

*

S.O.S. AMITIE

J'ai 14 ans et je cherche à correspondre avec filles et garçons de 14 à 18 ans. Thomas Janine BP 599 à Bouake. Côte d'Ivoire.

Recherche désespérément jeune homme de 15 à 18 ans pour jeune fille de 14 ans, joindre photo, réponse assurée, j'aime la moto, la musique et le cinéma. Barrier Isabelle, place de l'Eglise, 14810 Gonneville en Auge.

*

Je désire correspondre avec garçons et filles de mon âge, j'ai 16 ans. J'aime le sport, la musique, les sorties, le cinéma, joindre une photo si possible, réponse assurée. Corbin Magalie, au Bourg de Montereau, 45260 Lorais.

*

J'ai 16 ans et désire correspondre avec garçons de 16 à 20 ans, j'aime les sorties, la musique, l'équitation, le basket. . . Joindre une photo réponse assurée, gros bisous. Recousa Montserrat, rue des Jordils 19, 1400 Yverdon. Suisse.

J'ai 14 ans et je désire correspondre avec garçons ou filles de mon âge, parlant français ou anglais, j'aime Madonna. Delarue Estelle, 35 les Prés Fleuris, 28210 Nogent-le-Roi.

*

Je désire correspondre avec filles ou garçons de 13 à 14 ans, de tous les pays. J'aime le sport, la moto, les voyages, le cinéma, joindre photo si possible, réponse assurée. Torres Sylvie, 1 rue des Flandres, Dunkerque lotis la Rosière, 14880 Hermanville.

*

J'ai 14 ans et je désire correspondre avec filles et garçons de 13 à 16 ans, j'aime le cheval, le cinéma, les sorties et la musique, joindre une photo, réponse assurée. Sandrin Karine, 18 rue de Charles Bailleau, le Pin, 28120 Illiers Combray.

Pair work

Work with a partner who should sit opposite you. Partner B should turn to the next page.

Partner A

- It's 8 p.m. You and your partner are trying to decide what to watch on television. But what's on?
- You've got the programme for FR3 and your partner has the programme for C +.
- Discuss what's on and decide what you'll watch.
- Write down the times of the programmes you've decided to see.

Qu'est-ce qu'on pourrait voir?
A . . . . . . heures . . . . . . il y a des informations / un film etc.
Ça ne m'intéresse pas.
Ça a l'air │ bien.
　　　　　　│ pas mal.
Tu ne voudrais pas regarder ça?
D'accord. Alors, on voit . . . . . . jusqu'à . . . . . . heures
　　. . . . . . / et puis . . . . . . jusqu'à . . . . . . heures . . . . . . / c'est
　　ça?

20.05 FR3 BENNY HILL → 20.35
Série humoristique britannique. Sous-titrage Antiope.

20.35 FR3
MANIMAL → 21.20
Série américaine de Glen A. Larson, en huit épisodes. Réalisation : R. Mayberry. Rediffusion.

21.20 FR3 L'HOMME ET LA MUSIQUE → 22.20
Série de huit émissions de Yehudi Menuhin et Curtis W. Davis, avec Charles Weir. Réalisation : Richard Bocking et John Thomson. Précédente diffusion : 5.9.82.

22.20 FR3 SOIR 3 → 22.40

22.40 FR3 CINEMA DE MINUIT → 0.30
CYCLE CURIOSITES
DEUX FILLES AU TAPIS
Film américain de Robert Aldrich (1981), v.o.

Pair work

Partner B

- It's 8 p.m. You and your partner are trying to decide what to watch on television. But what's on?
- Your partner has the programme for FR3 and you have the programme for C +.
- Discuss what's on and decide what you'll watch.
- Write down the times of the programmes you've decided to see.

De . . . . . . heures . . . . . . à . . . . . . heures . . . . . . il y a des dessins animés / un film français etc.

Ça ne me tente pas.

Qu'est-ce qu'il y a d'autre?

Quelle horreur!

Je ne veux pas regarder ça.

Oui, je veux bien.

. . . . . . ça a l'air pas mal.

Tu ne veux pas regarder ça?

D'accord. C'est ce qu'on va faire.

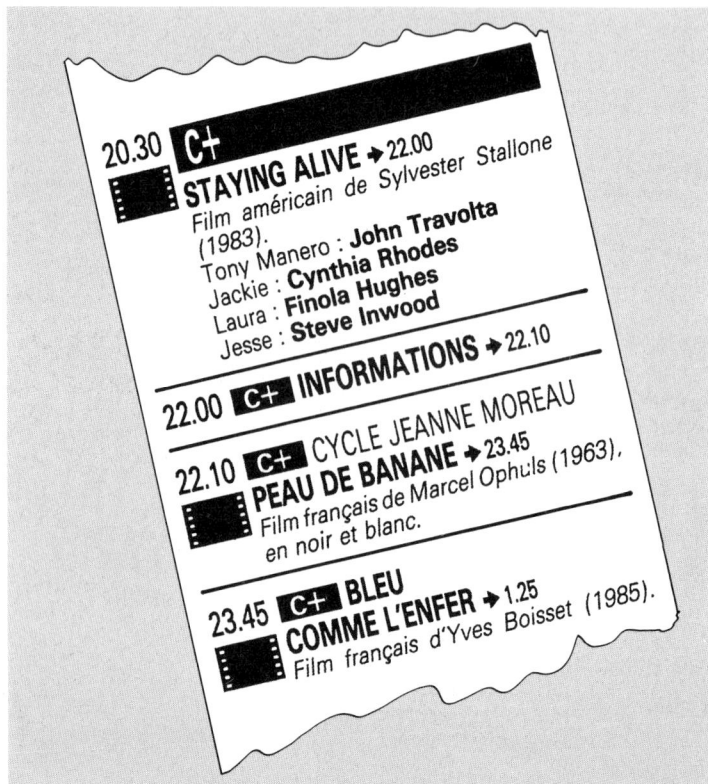

20.30 **C+** **STAYING ALIVE** → 22.00
Film américain de Sylvester Stallone (1983).
Tony Manero : **John Travolta**
Jackie : **Cynthia Rhodes**
Laura : **Finola Hughes**
Jesse : **Steve Inwood**

22.00 **C+** **INFORMATIONS** → 22.10

22.10 **C+** CYCLE JEANNE MOREAU
PEAU DE BANANE → 23.45
Film français de Marcel Ophüls (1963), en noir et blanc.

23.45 **C+** **BLEU COMME L'ENFER** → 1.25
Film français d'Yves Boisset (1985).

20 Pour fêter mes 17 ans

Bon anniversaire!

1 Listen to the three girls talking about how they celebrated their seventeenth birthday. Look at the pictures on your worksheet. Choose the one which goes with what each girl says and write her name beneath it.

REPROMASTER 20.1

2 Recopiez les phrases en remplissant les blancs:

a L'anniversaire de Catherine a lieu pendant . . . . . .
b Depuis qu'elle . . . . . . , elle fête son anniversaire à St-Malo.
c Ils . . . . . . en famille ce jour-là.
d Stéphanie . . . . . . en promenade avec la classe. Ils ont vu . . . . . .
e Le soir . . . . . .
f Claire a fait . . . . . .
g Son anniversaire, c'est . . . . . . , mais la soirée a eu lieu . . . . . .
h Ses bons amis sont arrivés à . . . . . . avec . . . . . .
i Ils avaient mis des bougies plus . . . . . .
j En arrivant ils lui sautaient au cou et ils disaient: . . . . . .
k Ses frères et ses amis ont pris . . . . . .

Un séjour à Sarzeau

You've taken a party of school-children to Sarzeau from 30th July to 11th August. They want a varied programme of sporting and cultural events. Look at the adverts below and write the programme for any five days of the holiday – in English. Give times if possible.

Try to present the programme in as attractive a way as you can.

Pair work

You're going to take it in turns to buy and sell things at the beach. Work with a partner who should sit opposite you. Partner B should turn to the next page.

Partner A

Buying:
- You decide to spend your birthday at the beach. But you have to get yourself kitted up first. Your partner runs the beach shop.
- Ask if he/she's got:

sun-glasses (des lunettes de soleil) swim-suits (des maillots de bain) straw hats (des chapeaux en paille) sun cream (de la crème solaire) rope-soled shoes (des espadrilles)

- Ask for the various items and work out how much it all comes to.

Vous avez du / de la / de l' / des . . . . . .?
Vous en avez en bleu / vert / rouge?
Je peux les voir?

J'en prendrai un / une en . . . . . . , s'il vous plaît.
C'est combien?
Je vous dois combien?

Selling:
- Now it's your turn to be the shop-keeper. Here are the things you're selling.

des boules: F24.60   des filets: F50.00

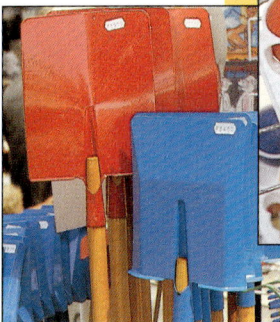

des pelles: F33.00

des ballons

des planches à vague

- If your partner asks to see them, swivel your book round for a moment!

Pair work

Selling:
- You are working in the beach-shop. Act out the conversation in which your partner buys things from you. Here are the things you're selling.

des maillots de bain

des espadrilles

des chapeaux en paille: F27.00

des lunettes de soleil: F50.00

- If your partner asks to see the things, swivel your book round for a moment!

Buying:
- Now it's your turn to do the buying. You're spending the day on the beach with your eight-year-old cousin.
- Ask the shop-keeper (your partner) what he or she has for a child of this age.
- Decide which items you want and ask for them.

Qu'est-ce que vous avez . . . . . . ?
Je peux voir?
Ils/elles sont à combien?
Je prends le/la rouge, bleu(e) à . . . . . . F, s'il vous plaît.
Je vous dois combien?

21 L'écossais version mini

Acheter des vêtements

Listen to the passage on the tape. Look at the different types of shirt in the pictures on your worksheet and write in the price of each on the ticket.

REPROMASTER
21.1

L'écossais ressort beaucoup cette année

You're responsible for the fashion page in your college magazine. Listen to the passage on the tape and write a paragraph in English describing what the French teenager will be wearing on the first day back at school this Autumn.

REPROMASTER
21.2

LES GRANDES TENDANCES MODE DE LA RENTRÉE

SEDUISEZ EN NOIR ET BLANC . . .

Et pour éviter le look trop classique, osez les mélanges des matières et des impressions. Chemisier à pois noirs, 175 F, 3 Suisses. Gilet à pressions vendu avec une jupe non photographiée, 625 F l'ensemble, Kookaï. Jupe pied-de-pouie, 240 F, Kookaï. Collant Le Bourget. Chaussettes, 49 F les 2 paires, La Blanche Porte. Ceinture, 125 F, 3 Suisses, Montre, 285 F, Kelton. Boucles d'oreilles, 1345 F, 3 Suisses. Chaussures, 169 F, Pile et Pull.

RENTRÉE

1 jupe
80% acrylique
10% polyester
10% autres fibres
du 13 au 16 ans
99 F
chemisier
65% polyester
35% coton
du 13 au 16 ans
145 F
bretelles
87% viscose
13% élastodienne
39 F
chaussettes hautes
60% acrylique
40% polyamide
29 F

2 blouson
100% polyamide
du 13 au 16 ans
350 F
pull
80% lambswool
20% polyamide
du 13 au 16 ans
145 F

3 sweat-shirt
50% coton
50% acrylique
du 13 au 16 ans
145 F
pantalon
100% coton
du 13 au 16 ans
220 F

4 pull
100% acrylique
du 13 au 16 ans
165 F
jean Lee Cooper
100% coton
du 13 au 16 ans
270 F

5 liquette
100% coton
du 13 au 16 ans
125 F
pantalon à bretelles
100% coton
du 14 au 16 ans
220 F

C&A

Lee Cooper

REPROMASTER
21.2

Pair work

Work with a partner who should sit opposite you. Partner B should turn to the next page.

Partner A

- You're selling the clothes in the photos below in the sizes indicated.
- Your partner wishes to buy certain things.
- Act out the conversation in which you discuss the colours and sizes available and complete the transaction.
- Work out how much it all comes to.

Tailles 36—38

Tailles 40—42—44

A taille unique

Tailles 40—42

Tailles 36—40—44

Tailles 40—42—44

Tailles 40—42—44

Vous le/la voulez	de quelle taille? de quelle couleur?
Oui, j'ai un / des	rayé / à pois / en gris / en coton / à manches longues / à manches courtes.

Mais | seulement en 36 et 38.
      | pas en 40.

Vous voulez l'essayer?
Lequel / laquelle prenez vous?
Ça vous fait . . . . . . F.

Pair work

Partner B

- It's hotter in France than you expected. You want to buy some summer clothes for yourself and your girl / boy friend, as illustrated below.
- The colour, size and maximum price you want to pay are written below each item.
- Ask the employee in the clothes' shop (your partner) whether he/she has got what you want and act out the conversation in which you buy the items. It's up to you to decide whether you will accept a smaller or larger size.
- Write down how much it all comes to.

LUI

Taille: 42

Couleur: gris / vert / bleu rayé
en coton
Prix maximum: 150F

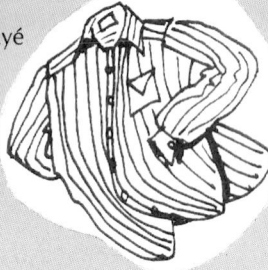

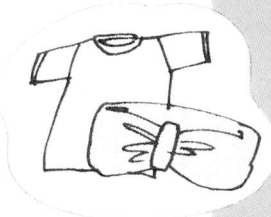

Couleur: Selon le choix
en polycoton
Prix maximum: 25F

Un tee-shirt ou un
bustier
Couleur: gris / vert
en coton
Prix maximum: 250F

ELLE

Taille: 38

Couleur: selon le choix
en coton
Prix maximum: 40F

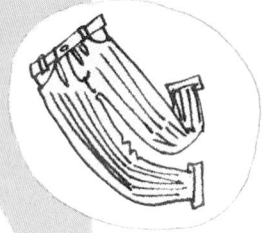

Un jean
Prix maximum: 200F

Couleur: blanc à pois verts
ou bleus
en tergal
Prix maximum: 30F

| Je voudrais | un pantalon / un jean / un chemisier à pois / un tee-shirt marin à manches longues / un tee-shirt marin à manches courtes. |

Qu'est-ce que vous avez comme couleurs?
Vous en avez en bleu / gris / vert etc?

Je peux l'essayer?
C'est combien?
Je m'excuse – c'est trop cher / étroit / grand.
Je le/la prends.
Je vous dois combien?

C'est pour moi. Je fais du 36/38/40/42/44
C'est pour mon ami(e). Il/elle fait du . . . . . .

22 La place est libre?

La ressemblance

Look at the picture on the next two pages. They form part of a picture story which appeared in the magazine **Intimité** – but they are in the wrong order. Put the pictures in the right order and rewrite the story in dialogue form.

Pair work

Work with a partner who should sit opposite you. Partner B should turn to the next page.

Partner A

- You keep leaving things on the bus / train / tube etc. You go and ask at the **bureau des objets trouvés** at the station.
- Look at the pictures and photos below which match up what you have lost and where you lost it.
- Ask the employee at the lost property office (your partner) whether your things have been handed in.
- Write a list of the things you manage to get back.

un k-way vert

un sac à dos vert

un carnet d'adresses

un porte-monnaie en cuir rouge

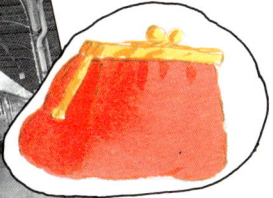

une écharpe bleue

un sac en plastique marqué Samaritaine.

J'ai perdu mon / ma . . . . . .
Je l'ai oublié(e) dans le/la . . . . . .
Il/elle est rouge / bleu(e) etc.

un appareil photo Pentax

Pair work

Partner B

- You work at the lost property office at the station. Your partner has lost several things.
- Search through the objects below. Each is labelled, saying where it was found. Ask where your partner lost the item, what colour or make it is and return it if it is his/hers.
- If not, apologise and say you haven't got it.

des gants en cuir noir: dans le car

un passeport britannique: dans la banque

un carnet d'adresses: dans une cabine téléphonique

un appareil photo Pentax: dans un taxi

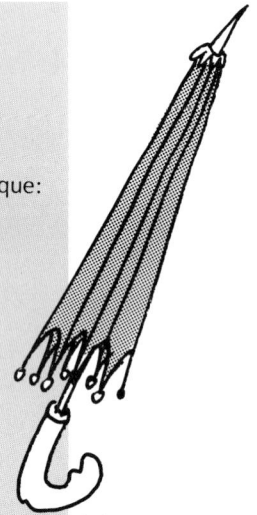

un parapluie: dans le train

un sac en plastique marqué Samaritaine: dans le car 52 en direction de Mettray

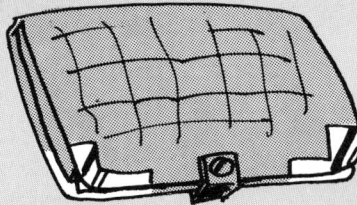

un porte-monnaie en cuir noir: dans la station-service

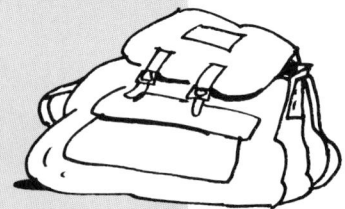

un sac à dos vert: dans le métro

Vous l'avez perdu(e), où?
Il/elle est de quelle couleur / de quelle marque?
Oui, je l'ai. Voilà.
Non, désolé(e), je ne l'ai pas.

- Write a list of the items you still have on your hands at the lost property office.

La carte jeune

REPROMASTER
22.1

1 Listen to the **employé** at the station in Figeac explaining
  about the **carte jeune** and fill in the information on your
  worksheet.

2 Listen to the passage once more and write out the
  sentences below, filling in the blanks:

   a . . . . . . nous renouvelons ce produit.
   b Elle donne droit à . . . . . . à faire . . . . . .
      qu'il veut.
   c On a . . . . . . de réduction sur le tarif
      normal . . . . . . commencer le voyage en
      période bleue.
   d Son prix est . . . . . .
   e D' . . . . . . , sur la . . . . . . de Dieppe à
      Newhaven, elle donne droit à . . . . . .
   f Elle donne également droit à une
      réduction sur . . . . . .
   g Elle donne droit . . . . . . sur un train de
      nuit.
   h Alors, ... , la période bleue, c'est du
      . . . . . . c'est-à-dire . . . . . .

23 Passe de bonnes vacances

Il faisait très, très chaud

1 Look at the photos below and listen to Claire talking about them on the tape. Decide which order they should be in. Write the numbers 1–3 in a column on a piece of paper and write a, b, or c beside each number.

A

B

C

2 Terminez les phrases suivantes:

a Claire dit que la photo prise avec ses frères est 'assez rigolote' parce que . . . . . .

b Les deux jeunes filles ont enlevé leurs bouées de sauvetage parce que . . . . . .

c Claire aime bien la photo prise avec Mélanie parce que . . . . . .

Pair work

Work with a partner who should sit opposite you. Partner B should look at his/her worksheet.

Partner A

- You've got the information your partner needs to plan his/her holiday. Look at the extracts from the F.U.A.J. (Youth Hostelling Association) booklet below and give the information required:

ESCALADE
LA PALUD-SUR-VERDON
ALPES HAUTE PROVENCE

ESCALADE

PERFECTIONNEMENT. Minimum 16 ans.
DUREE: 5j.(F2)
PRIX: 1.950 F (PC)
DATES: 20.7-24.7 ● 10.8-14.8

PROGRAMME: Les stages se déroulent du lundi matin au vendredi soir. Ils s'adressent aux grimpeurs déjà confirmés. Niveau demandé: IV + à V + Travail en moulinette, passage en libre, en tête et en sécurité, afin d'arriver à "faire" les grandes voies classiques du Verdon.

EQUITATION
ARRENS
HAUTES-PYRENEES

RANDONNEE EQUESTRE EN MONTAGNE

TOUS NIVEAUX. Minimum 14 ans.
DUREE: 6 j. (F I) PRIX: : I. 850 F (PC)
DATES: 21.6-28.6 ● 28.6-05.7 ● 05.7-12.7 ● 12.7-19.7 ● 26.7-02.8 ● 02.8-09.8 ● 09.8-15.8
+ I semaine durant les congés scolaires de la Toussaint.

PROGRAMME: Sur des chevaux dociles et résistants, une randonnée dépaysante dans une montagne encore préservée. Minimum 6 heures de cheval par jour. Coucher en gîte, cabane de berger, sous tentes.

FARNIENTE
CHAMROUSSE ISERE

"APPRENDRE A NE RIEN FAIRE"

TOUS NIVEAUX. Minimum 14 ans.
DUREE: 7 j. (F I)
PRIX: 700 F (PC)
DATES: 28.6-05.7 ● 05.7-12.7 ● 12.7-19.7 ● 19.7-26.7 ● 26.7-02.8 ● 02.8-09.8 ● 09.8-16.8

PROGRAMME: Programme sur mesure, à partir des envies de chacun. Logement en chambres de 2 ou 3 avec douches. Soirée animée par les séjournants. Pour les fous de l'activité, ski d'été, delta-plane, parapente, tennis, équitation, piscine etc . . .

l'équitation horse-riding
une randonnée a ride
dépaysant spectacular
les soins aux chevaux grooming, looking after your horse
cols et crêtes passes and peaks
gîte house, (often) converted farm buildings
l'escalade rock-climbing
se dérouler to take place
les grimpeurs confirmés experienced climbers

les grandes voies classiques great classic routes
sur mesure adapted to individual taste
leurs disponibilités financières how much money they've got!
soirée animée par les séjournants participants make their own evening entertainment
le parapente jumping off hills with steerable parachutes

Hello Sarah

Read the letter below and write a suitable reply.

Hello Sarah,

Je passe mes vacances à Erquy dans les Côtes-du-Nord. Il fait très beau. J'ai fait la connaissance de beaucoup de jeunes de mon âge. Ils sont tous super sympas mais il y en a un qui m'intéresse plus que les autres. Il s'appelle Marc, il a 17 ans, les yeux bleus, les cheveux bruns, enfin tu vois il est super.

Le matin je fais de la voile, j'adore ça. Le seul inconvénient c'est qu'il faut se lever tôt. Et toi, comment vas-tu? Comment se passent tes vacances? Bon voilà, je te laisse en espérant recevoir très vite de tes nouvelles.

À bientôt,   Séverine

P.S. Passe de bonnes vacances.

faire la **connaissance de** to get to know
le seul inconvénient the only disadvantage